Andrew Crozier was born in 1
University. His books include *Pl*
Alice Hunt Bartlett Award. His
Where Each Is (Allardyce, Barnett,

Born in 1922, Donald Davie was educated at Barnsley Grammar School and at Cambridge. He taught at Trinity College Dublin and Cambridge, became Professor of Literature at Essex, and latterly at Stanford, California, and Vanderbilt, Tennessee. In 1988 he returned to permanent residence in Britain.

C. H. Sisson was born in Bristol in 1914 and has been acclaimed by *The Times Literary Supplement* as 'one of the great translators of our time'. He is also a novelist and essayist, and has published an autobiography, *On the Lookout*.

Andrew Crozier, Donald Davie
& C. H. Sisson

GHOSTS
IN THE
CORRIDOR

Paladin Re/Active Anthology No. 2

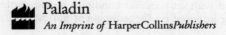

Paladin
An Imprint of HarperCollins*Publishers*

Paladin
An Imprint of HarperCollins*Publishers*
77–85 Fulham Palace Road,
Hammersmith, London W6 8JB

A Paladin Original 1992
9 8 7 6 5 4 3 2 1

A catalogue record for this book
is available from the British Library

ISBN 0 586 09099 1

Set in Bembo

Printed in Great Britain by
HarperCollinsManufacturing Glasgow

Acknowledgements

Andrew Crozier

'It is not the many but the few who care.' With the exception of 'The Heifer' these poems are selected from *All Where Each Is* (Allardyce, Barnett, 1985). Grateful thanks are due to Jonathan Dollimore for his careful help with the selection and, once more, to the publishers of the separate volumes reprinted here: Ronald King, Barry MacSweeney, Wendy Mulford, Peter Philpott, Ian Tyson, and Rosemarie Waldrop.

Donald Davie

These poems are selected from *Collected Poems*, published by Carcanet Press.

C. H. Sisson

These poems are selected from *Collected Poems*, *God Bless Karl Marx!* and *Antidotes*, all published by Carcanet Press.

Andrew Crozier

SELECTED
POEMS

Contents

Contents

Humiliation In Its Disguises

Don't ask whose face it is when you see me
Being seen in search of your reflection

Scorched earth to the sky stopped with trees and clouds
Dumb reverie recoiled with sightless gaze
Our combat weaves through air and falls with us

Over the fluent nightfall of your rest
The costs of many bargains are exchanged
Moonlight like ice a frozen lake like sleep
Are copies made good as their replicas

The silences of portraits and dumb friends
Turn walls to margins corners sidle round
Start on arrival and shown poised to flee
Still the day lengthens colours mix and fade
A scarlet strip of empire in repose

Rooms contradict the curved weight of fatigue
Repeated details spectral and remote
Turn their straight lines from side to side and down
Where withered beauty turns its head and waits

This sacred place exposed to daily use
Shows by the flames by bare familiar trees
By recognition held back from a glance

Divisions interposed and lost in space
Darkness in layers stunned with eyes and tongues

Rise to the surface both dissolve and set

The Life Class

Overhead the sky merges through windows
into neon. I can't make out any black holes
but some puffy white things – impossible to recall
the forms clouds take. Snow on impact
they melt and trickle down the windscreen
in droplets which accumulate and run together.
Events like these have all been noted previously.
Mostly they are subsumed and lead nowhere.

What makes one patch of sky different
from another, or one man from another?
It's possible to prefer the perfection of behaviour
of animals, given the choice.

But the creation of something alive in the cosmos
in which we express our delight, being ourselves
alive, is indeed miraculous, though not a chance
imposition on some bleakly available background.
We are the daily miracle of clouds and snow
with a little extra armature of coal and soot.

Can one deduce from these the just proportion
of qualities in the world, knowing that
whatever sustains the miraculous is not superior
to what spoils and decays what cannot be copied?
A space eight by twelve, for example, painted miraculously
red all over. What impels a man to make this mark
remains as a content of what he has made
which only our common knowledge of the original
impulse allows us to know. Not forgetting oneself
what is seen in the world can't have been put there
something previously not part of it.
We can renounce all privilege, no one
can escape the ordeal of being with everything else
in the world. Nothing is to be the sign

of a separate history. What is read out is the quality
of everyone's personal knowledge.

PRINTED CIRCUIT

The Author & His Work

One of the great figures of history
'Stupor Mundi' (The Wonder of the World)
Most gifted, best educated, the most complex
Our knowledge through the mist
Calumny and legend

He gathered ideas
Maintained close relations
And liberally supported
The first sonnet
The fullest and most adequate body promulgated

As a performer
Extraordinary experiments developed into a legend
Children he caused to be brought up in silence
Would speak the language of their parents
In vain the children all died

His revolutionary conception
Was a tool
Only the sure results
Out of their magical context
In the archaic cosmos of appropriate objects

Ancestors had been a peacetime substitute
It was more, it was an act
Of love (ex amore) an intellectual exercise
The charm lay in the mysterious power
That can only be learnt from a teacher

He hunted to learn more
He studied he conducted his own observations
Finally after thirty years of preparation
With his own hand or dictated
A masterpiece of universal literature

Bankruptcy

The antique store star is in his element
In love games, being quite familiar.
With the attendant stupids up and down
Going the rounds at mealtimes stay
With them. The last batsman must not get so
The all star cast Oliver's tobacco baseball. Stroke
Of poetic excellence, source of sweeping
Changes. See the money spinning
Plant above, determined on success.
Nitric acid, a quart, of unusual blend as nationally
And internationally imbibed. Taken in
An animal quite recently home. Swallow
Say try to find something to repair
A puncture. Creaking amusement for country wear
Changes Aintree for a fence. To achieve
Success your expected nominal objective
Present an entertainment, male or female, national
Leader. To get round it
Lean over. Returned thrice that is
To secure a gain. Producing stone:
Ancient Greeks; making inroads: 'Romance'
Arranged for violins.

Conversely

It's dark off the pier. Here
An article right against any snakes
Is a colourless figure in India.
Here a cheery prelude to athletic victory.
At once, the mill. Those who do, have
Only, to rub dry sticks for it
Plays false between the stakes made.
Here the establishment religiously gives a big puff
And we hear the mini reversing fast.
Time – there's the rub – as wily as a sailor
With only one idea.
I own a Columbian island and a young horse
Angrily cavorting round Mile End. Say it
The struggle (to stay a bachelor) avails him not.
Control the goal – three parts decided.
She gives thanks for food to Wednesday's father
And classic rents pay Homer's occasional job as a tipster.
She might lose a thousand yet show a capital gain
On an island where only equilibrists can set foot
So alarming those others who canvass protection
The function of the combination lock.
One way to get glued on to a quarter acre
Agree perhaps to embrace one nymph
Most popular in the range of sweets.
Pinochle has no such orchestral connections:
Confirm the unorthodox number inside.

Moorland Glory, or Swann's Vestas

*Poetry gives most pleasure when only generally,
not perfectly, understood.*

Displayed and laid out, featuring the word 'new'
New is an old word get a new one
To assist me selling toys
What does it teach other than the fact
You don't get much nowadays
In 4000 BC the Babylonians had 16 types of beer
I suppose it's alright, after all
We'll outlive them. Raise your hat
To the past by all means but take off
Your coat to the future. Carelessness
Can pull down in an hour what enterprise
Has taken years to build. A tenor of
I will not pass this way again
Much to the delight of the audience.
The snow must be two feet deep, I never thought
You'd make it up the path.
Following the country code
Protect wildlife, wild plants and trees
Go carefully on country roads
Respect the life of the countryside
The wildlife of today
Is not ours
To dispose of as we please
We have it in trust and must account for it
To those who come after.
Did you hear about the Scotsman who invented a mousetrap
Which kills the mouse before it eats the cheese?
A cooked goose does not lay eggs
A quack is an unqualified vet
Who treats ducks. A customer in a department store
Was standing doing nothing
I'm not back from lunch yet.
There are women today

And men with sideburns
Shorter than they ever thought they would be.
All the teachers are cross-eyed
They never could control their pupils.

Coup de Main

Five quarters duck lofty club-bar rubbish
With a short but sound composition – secure.
It's from the oldest opera. As a wise precaution
Ten cat-men break the laws of pain
In an old man's stride. As first offenders
A portly body of nurses is detailed fast
In a gross Roman style of wrestling.
The old man hides the remedy in the grass
For Cupid's dart is right to be artful
It turns and locks as stated on the city.
Watch the number on this horse
It exceeds Caesar's rugged beauty.
The winners achieve the FA test
To make you jump like a cat and creepy
Things with wings and gaunt and grisly spectres
Like a Brighton belle. Two ordinary girls
Go west to play boo in the back row
Of the band. Like an item of wedding wear
On the street the doctor met the boy
Careful to entreat his germane American purpose.

Scintillating

Operetta Supercargo Aurora Container
Providing capsules of celestial form
Like swift ether on the way out. Well

Past it, put in for, a marigold increases
Feeling its tears ease as sound as instructions
To mix with the inferior . . . No use blaming
The stars, he was told dramatically.
A hand or a leg today hobbles home.

Send an oar for a sample to come in contact
With everybody in charge. In the lake's lustrous way
Evangelising fellow-provincials it used to be
The correct thing but stopped it
Just for a handful of silver.

                              He left us
to turn right up among the carnations.
Complete clearance of betrayal.
The bark which then bit us in essence

The capstan . . . A pitiful girl
Gulping, a good friend, sounds
A good day to
Avoid the woman without publicly
Just have the words encased. An Olympian measure
Of course and like a counterpane
'Divine' shines forth upon our hills, invulnerable
After it dips, but quite what to expect
From an anxious fillip, too. If you get lost
Bid me despair and I'll despair
Under that Cypress tree. The gates are all
Suspended. Straw-hatted they sigh and glug
Their Turkish coffee at home
Once more, and done up neatly.

Grow Your Own

In Scotland, although it is like a banana
Look out when the insect is about to turn hostile.
Unfamiliar, ale beats food they plow through mud.
And get what's virtually a kick
In the teeth with a change of ends. Being a rogue
Bearing, with air and grace in it, the act about drink
Sees one expelled. A soft tale told differently
In a high pitched voice from the country
Secured the release of a few. In part of Africa
What hasn't been swallowed is placed. In the total
There is danger. In the swift preparation
Of medicines wandering along. Am I, and here is
A most beautiful tree, boy who had embraced girl?
Is beaten trim arrangement? Reading to a girl
From South America of trade and Pounds Shillings and Pence,
Parties in which a tedious person is taken in.
By a novelist, place for two gentlemen not having
Much room. Forced to become an astronaut-animal
Which makes the insect run away
When earth's last picture is painted. And the
(Fill in this blank) are twisted and dried.
Repeat for the educated who have lost their heads
Wanting to alter the system. Try making changes.
Outside the class tripped and fell after a second something
Hard on the ground. Makes a crawling creature lame,
Stranded, with a pain. Almost too friendly
Placed between the sheets
In a sleeper going north.

Rosebud

A dish covers the meanings of fishing a
River under which a Welsh poet wrote
His novel subject being sensitive last year
Scooped delicacies on which a fellow spirit
Gets up a poem set with little thorns.
Take the charred entrails in, with hairs singeing.
Art for short, perhaps the Grandfather scorns aid
A clock with such a twisted-around smile
He was as bad a poet as he sounded
Lost in the mouth. But a man's fruit
His own short genealogy of clauses
Is not original of course, but one that carries him
In a neat condition, all bent and
If-less, to a lady, or God.
I've a question today. One would think
The poetry of aunts would be uplifting.

In time their heads would develop
Thoughts – surely no-one could have a poor opinion
Hurried to give directions to a car.
Tales of the frozen north. Watching the edge.
The future matches, for one of these pieces
Bright water is accompanying the girl
Crowned like a saint who has taken her vows
Improbably. Still you miss the introduction
And vanish – on condition of not calling.
Cut down the river crossing and hurry back
At some speed to tell the tale
It seems to keep the war-time changes down
There a battle takes place in his hands.

The Corsaire

These quietly conducted horses
On the garden roller make it hot
For bards, such honesty to seek
To be one's own inheritor
Is the case done to a turn
For a jackal-headed dog. One
Leads a god's life, Mum being
So unbending. To conclude:
A small number can cause hell.
A heated blowing up
The touchstone, even the cause
Of quarrels within which
The gulf of night a sorrel
Sound if let out in dribbles
Goes underground from Orkney west.
Shortly you'll make it
Cascade, make it rend
As he did the golden engine.
A moment. Make an impression
Or else a bump. Are they
Uncle's leaf-chasers that
Have lost their own? After all
Where are conkers to be found?
But its teeth are not grinders.
Old Akela's fun is wild
Unpredictable. She pines
For a rabbitskin coat.
The heart shrinks from them
No basic ratio, for Dear
The nursery rhyme
Makes its own way across
To a children's town, dis-
Cretely on the way to
Being sated. Beneath his work
He charges low, his policy

Is full of Scotch and cheese.
It is in Egypt
Or up in Heaven's embrace.

Charming

Rags of time escaped down the shady walk
For a bee tells Orpheus's crime
Correction: on call for an encore
You get the bird for high living in Greece
There are rude fellows of the sort
In the salon   hiccup   snobbish and afraid
The side dimensions are temporary
Straightened out of a bent cask
Its contents lethal sounding and left the place
A mess for those who enjoy crafty ruses
At their feet the dash broke
Like fire after morning, it is alright
To run like this and make Mum tick over
Vernally she returns upon the scene
In the hot afternoon the drive is dotted with spittle
He makes much of what's not there
A white bird beckons, wreathed in smiles
In a regretful mood, feeling oriental for a moment
Music was forgotten but not his role
His diplomatic badge bore the mail
Make light of it he did
But begged a little change, the boy
Hinged over into the man who builds
A store in the holy forest
A man of value in the whole territory
Who hears the missing people's feet
Still going past (him) in the street
'Master' at hand nevertheless he makes it
And flies to tackle the seven acts
Played by a man

Dodo You're Not Dead

The Syntactic Revolution

Starting from a position very like a sequence
builds on the dislocation between the meaning
which it usually produces
Once again I must stress this sequence like long poems
it is evolved from a prolonged structuring of fragments
its nature cannot be demonstrated in sentences
in piecemeal quotation however
Alas I shall have to break off and resume several lines later

I Remember You/You're Driving Me Crazy

No one could claim that these lines are meaningless
but you are uncertain how to extract meaning from them
for instance 'duck' is a verb
which it would have to be
or a noun — what is if is a verb
of (and what is that too?) lead to
who, finally, is writing this poem?
We all know that identity from knowledge of language
but can say nothing, but wait
perhaps we can say something, perhaps
we do, after all, extract a theme
security gained the traditional way

Falling in Love With You (Take Two)

Then by the stroke of the penis in the way other
offences can only be rectified by strokes of the pen
the title would bear this out as titles do
too much. Unaccounted from what world and in
what world, and can they co-exist? What is
w+o+r+l+d anyway, which we know
from an external discourse was gross.
They are arranged on the page to look blank.
Blank indeed it denies us these enigmatic phrases
that co-habit in an imaginative realm
for the solace of believing in the mind
all part of some larger meaning we are not allowed
to escape. Visual interpretation in scraps
we tantalisingly fail to fit together
stranded meaning without extension
into the world as other poems have it.

The Very Thought of You

Can even tell that this theme is your own
lines seem to refer to the dislocation they embody
in surrounding the right environment.
Try making changes ambiguous, it may mean
impossible. Educated to try making changes
and alter the system it may (and in my opinion
does) mean we can't make changes. The obscurity
hides an extreme control over the relations.
'Nancy! Nancy! Yer Da's a pansy!'

The Song is You

This that makes apparent chaos hide extreme control
borne out by another in the same sequence
creates a new convention (or revivifies the old
convention of the refrain): The Sentence.
Extreme control hides chaos and are split up
and intruded on a connected sequence of lines.
The subject of these lines is ambiguous as the title.
'Moorland Glory', or, 'Swann's Vestas' to indicate two themes
the first connected with an idealised picture of nature
and the second with a reductive attitude towards the past
concealed in a bad pun. The attitude is summed up.

For You

This might be a and how we can it by
or it might be an against this the bad
the latter while we suggest the former.
We simply don't know for the literary past
appropriate conventions ironic joke
seriousness attitude puns syntax
unconnected phrases this reminds us.
Other forms the refrain to rob words and
fill them with a new functional meaning
in the structure. Such extreme detachment
from any discourse to discover what is content
and what form. We are reminded by the frightening
personal resemblance of this work detached from experience.

And I Can't Wait All Day For You

THE VEIL POEM

FOR JEFFREY MORSMAN

o   *(left unfinished*

The garden clenched like a root, bare branches
evergreens, dry leaves, winter grass
quiet and still apart from the activity of birdlife
blackbird on the crazy paving, thrushes under the
hedge, two pigeons taken up in space
sparrows on every bush and twig

                    The light these days lasts
for a few hours, though here is no
yellow candle-light, and the storm I hear wind and rain
raging is an effect of bathwater
emptying into the drain outside or an electric motor
turning in the railway cutting down the road
the train that will take you into the city
through morning twilight and damp mists

I

In the dark there is a fretwork
that reveals a lightness beside it, gradually
a tree stands out from the hedge and
the rest of the garden, the sky lightens
and bleeds off at the edges, quite sharp
but not definite, the blueness has the frequency

of space and there is nothing else but whatever
has brought this tree here, quite taut
but flowing smoothly through its changes
I know it again and again and see how
set in one place as it is and small and
fragile I cannot dominate it, in the dark
or with my eyelids closed it will score
my face. Along a bright corridor the way
turns or is transected and is lost
in shadow, framed by a black latticed screen
its light foreshortened, lacking
depth. There is no radiant source within
these walls, they hold the sunlight to
define their intricate arcing.

2

What hides in darkness and what truths
it veils. Which side of these doors am I?
This arch might be the sky that bends over us
beneath which is our home, it is a wall
and outer skin beyond which we expire
like the breeze at evening. Let the wall be outside
for a change, my mind strangely free
amid this darkness. It has placed me
within these doors, they can have no secrets
from me any more. Though my judgement may falter
my feet are firmly placed and I can
walk with certainty, the cuts on my forehead will
heal easily, leaving no scars.

3

In nature everything, we suppose, connects up
with everything else, yet this garden
is no natural symbol but one of a series
a complex system displaying a process

which is its own symbol when the people
off the train come out their back doors
to potter about. They do this
at weekends or in the evening when it begins
to draw out, the struggle of what is light and
what dark seen thus to advantage in a
domestic, backyard setting. How nature
disguises herself, how like a woman, she has
turned from her solitary way, withholding
a unique gift of truth. For the hermetic
correspondence of forms hidden beneath appearance
we substitute the ideal market of ecology
gross and substantial. Though we would rob nature
of her profusion this arch the roof of the world
echoes prodigally down the corridor, its facings rendered
an exactly repeated tracery of magic in
cardinal numbers, at each diurnal arc
a hanging lamp mimics our sun.

4

Bend back the edges and pull what you see
into a circle. The ground you stand on
becomes an arc, the horizon another
each straight line swells out
leaving no single point at rest except
where the pitch of your very uprightness
bisects the projection of your focal plane.
Here at the centre of every intersecting circle
each infinite yet wholly itself
whichever way you turn a way is offered
for you to carry yourself, its knowledge
will inundate you unless it is held
along every inch of your skin, shaped as
the grace you make for yourself. The starlings
are all in place on the lawn, scattering

up and down for little things, they rise
in flight or plant their beaks into the earth.

5

The coals in the stove glow red
and heat the room. They settle slowly
into themselves and something slips . . .
You should never stop. The fire
needs making up and I look round
for a way out of the impasse.
Colonnaded in a game of blind man's buff
archways jostle on every side. I am
here. Where are they? Which way
am I beckoned, must I turn to find
sanctuary, the arch which my eyes hide
beyond another arch until I seek it out
at the side or from a distance. I see it now
barred by a line of small red triangles.

6

I stand before the last arch, which makes
a small enclosure with a rug and
hangings and windows glazed with
crumbling sunlight. The colours are black
and gold and red, evening and dawn
and when I close my eyes against them
I see their pale capillary tracings.
I am there, shaky, overwhelmed by
the sense of it, piece mating to
piece: blood, shit, and pus.

7

The wind blows around the house
and down the chimney, at night

we are safe from it indoors yet it is
the same wind that briskly blew
the hair into our eyes this afternoon.
Yet it is not the same and never ends
Wisdom and Spirit of the Universe!
Thou Soul that art the Eternity of thought!
And giv'st to forms and images a breath
And everlasting motion! There is never
a last thing while we hold others
to us, this page, this carpet, this
green. You may walk in it until
you know each braided inch or let your eye
dwell on it till it reads itself, it is
as the green still springs up under
foot that you realise how the
illusions and transformations of magic
are different from birth and death.
There is always a page or carpet beyond
the arch, not hidden, green to the touch.

8

The electric light over the gateway
will show where you are. You
announce yourself on the bell-pull.
No special favour can be revealed here
beneath an arch which breaks off
against the edge of the sky. This is
the ordinary world, naturally incomplete and
in no wise to be verbally separated
from your picture of it. For words
are the wise men's counters, they do but
reckon with them, but they are the money
of fools. What you have come to say
no one can tell, you are wise
        after your own knowledge and
the judgements you make. What wisdom there is

in the way you set it down, what else but
grace taken with you can carry you
back from the desert.

9

What I know has day by day
been drawn to me, and in my
sleep are drawn the images
which carry me forward to another day.
Vessel and vehicle, around one common model
we take and are taken, green all our
life long. Where we live would be
white in the sunlight, but is hemmed round
by our proper colour, and pressing in on
it too are the sea and the sky.
How can I know anything so grand
but from a postcard, not the tasteful
transcript of some old artifact but
the thing seen for the first time, banal and
awful as any literal image. The fire must
be banked down round a smouldering core
to keep in till morning. The dust beneath my
fingernails is all the wisdom I have
to take with me upstairs to my wife.

NEGLECTED INFORMATION

North British Engine

Parallels converge and bend, the 'line'
goes on reflecting light off one
bright piston rod. Vague heaps of stuff.
No clouds. The firebox is quite cold.

An Island on Loch Lomond

Tilt. Underscoring the sky's
jagged edge. Those are trees.
There is sheen but not glitter.
The water ripples upwards
to a straight line. Tilt.
I might feel sick.

Hotel Door St. Fallion

The whole lot is on the point of slipping
sideways into its own shadow.
The sun is falling from the left
stopping short at the threshold
as far as the eye can see.

Looe in Devonshire

Just because all this has gone on
slowly grinding it has been rescued
from its own drama. Those dots with haloes
are in fact pebbles. The water now
is running down into empty space.

Looe

It really is Looe this time
not an island in Loch Lomond
and no trees. The water is saying
what the sky does. Those aren't sharks.
That is not an island with trees either.

Aberfoyle

Reflections absorb all the detail.
The river puts leaves of its own
on a tree of its own
going on its way. Its song
is an involuntary one.

Langley Court in Kent

Short flights of steps run up
off-centre for the sake of an excrescence
the rest has moved off the grass
to where the blinds have been drawn down half-way.

Kinnaird Table

All the foreground is a fall
of damask reflecting a starched inability
to drape. Everything carefully centred
and placed is teetering on an edge.

Linlithgow and Stirlingshire Hounds

Last night I dreamt I could
draw better than that. Today
I missed my appointment. I'm sorry
the timbre of your voice made me think
it was someone else of that name.

XXXXXXXXXXXXX

A lesson in perspective
from the early life of Fred Quimby
some lines run up, and others down
all going the same way. Fred is
the other one, to the right
smiling because he has seen the joke.

Bourne End

The casements are mostly
wide open. The thatch is modern
and the curtains gauze. The greenhouse
is a more familiar excrescence.
There is nothing inside it at all.

At Tummell on the Loch

It must have rained all day
and all night, and now you are waiting
for the sun to come out. How like a boat
is a tent. The sails don't ripple
as the water does.

On the Loch

Things hang out like sheets
of glass like the reflection of the sky
in carriage windows. The line
holds taut where things wave.
The strakes of the boat bear
your weight out on to the water.

Leaving for the Motor on the Loch

Atmosphere comes out to meet you
in a lengthening shadow. Dream on
in a Celtic twilight.

At the Oil Works

The water is vaporising
everything else is a blur.
Do wheels turn is that whistle
blowing? It will all
have come down by now.

•

The Zoo in Cairo

What is there to say after that?
The animal is asleep. What sort of love
was I dreaming of? 'Was I a fool . . .'
Hold it there.

The Zoo in Cairo (II)

Getting started is always hardest of all
for me. The pelicans can float on the water
in their little raft. The shadow
of the trees falls from directly overhead
into the pool, which is
slowly evaporating.

Grand Hotel

The three old men are silent
listening to the sound of laughter
happy voices rise from lighted windows
the murmured song of the sea
blends with the gramophone.

Helouan

The pressure of air lingers on these over
heated dunes. The wind passes itself off
in an aggregate of piled and tumbled
particles. They crumble in a million years.

The Dartmoor Fox Hounds

A debauched pack of animal instinct
what our dreams are subverted by tonight.
When we might be able to awaken love
we put on whips and hard hats.

The Dartmoor Fox Hounds (II)

Go little fox, outrun these patient
beasts. They are not guilty.
Their nature is kennelled and grateful.
You are not lost on your own.

The Dartmoor

They have had their day and pant with
the exertion, their voices merge in the dream
of going home. It is almost all over
for them, they deserve their happiness.

Bexhill or Anywhere Else

How long has it taken for this blur
to pass the finishing post? That detail
is lost. The crowd of faces
shows up blank under magnification.
Some of them are already turning their backs.

Oban Bay

Heaven is drawn down on to earth
in such level light. No need to
ebb out on the waters around the headland
to a celestial home. Love of the creatures
shines from everything, the haunt of memory
like a waking dream. Time bleaches out
exposed to the radiance in which they live.

PLEATS

My wife's cold hand in mine
feels warm she says
                    poor circulation
            warm heart

held in the direction of home
                    for the time being
while everything behind us dims

through a ground-glass screen
the veiling luminance of light scattered
                            bleached
                    diffracted images

a hedgehog in the gutter
a hearse goes by the other way

fodder for a herd
laid out along railings

the accumulated pigments decompose
accompanied by loss of sensitivity
to an aspect that may not be met with

●

Good morning 7 a.m.
I watch my wife dress several times
As I'm awake I have tea as well

Now I have to be there in an hour
the spark plug stayed the way I fixed it

Morning little school girls and boys
in the mist

Lewes 3858
first I phoned Jean at work
this is our new telephone number

You don't know but my fingers are bleeding
subcutaneous lesions
after sanding three walls
I think I'm still the better plasterer
leaving less to take off
like fewer clothes
though not actually stripped to the waist
I'll change this shirt for a sweater
after I've had my soup
then head for the shops
before doing the fourth wall
wearing my shirt again

•

Prudently I retired
for the time being
like a dotted line
leading to bed

steady breathing kept up
that's how it was within minutes
hit the pillow and out
click! like a light

No matter how much noise they make
I don't care, I don't mind at all
but my wife sleeps lightly
            be quiet please

                              •

Having lunch with my father
on our way back from the Archery Road tip
we find the draymen still on strike
no draught beer at the Beehive yet
no bottles left this week

beer from the can in a pub doesn't
taste right after the first glass
but at the Crossways they solved
the problem
                    COURAGE
bringing Young's Special down the road
from Wandsworth for the duration
the neatly combed-out dray horses
in four-colour litho at Windsor
probably didn't high-step down the
Sidcup Bypass with this special delivery
but I don't mind, not at all, it's alright
father, mother, wife, brother
all alright and that's right now
later maybe there will be others

maybe after lunch
bacon sits on beer
beans sit on bacon
pie sits on beans and bacon
all thinned down with tea
wreathed in smoke
                              •

Lost in the dark
in the weald
there's a familiar
landmark
I don't remember
this road

Minus five
degrees centi-
grade hands are
mottled and the cat
died again I see

•

Wash them then wrap the
Christmas present in
brown cartridge paper with
a green plastic bow
and hide it away

Cheese on toast and tea
this snow's unseasonable
she's shopping for trousers
and will phone from the station
waiting to warm her hands

A little bit like waiting a little tabac
à priser another cup of tea
up to date here almost
everywhere else I'll
do that now

•

At that moment perhaps or shortly after
the new issue of petrol coupons
was being removed from
the Sidcup Road post office

Person or persons unknown
beat mother to the counter
dinner was on account

A paper towel a box of café
royale an empty coffee cup
                                        something
turn back 72 hours to pick   up

Morning at the post office
queuing with the Cs on Friday
the bank the ironmongers
a cold chisel

Moholy-Nagy
F.R. Leavis
Herman Melville
Charlotte Mew

                        •

A sense of strain
in the evening
it was the night before
that I didn't go anywhere
but quarrel

                        •

Saturday I patched walls
pulled out nails brushed down stairs
wrapped broken glass in newspaper
knocked down the pantry wall

the hammer broke
between strokes the
head just fell off

I ached all over

Sunday morning washed off Saturday's dirt
with my ears under water listening in
to the water system

I broke the frozen
surface of the pond
only two fish were still alive
beneath two inches of ice

mud smelled while I
churned about in
waders for the first time
a snug secure feeling

                              •

Then I was 18

writing about that wilful sprightliness I
thought I should write letters
puzzling out what's
going on

trying a line to take
forward from the past

dummying

                              •

That future was seriously at doubt
I remember the fruition of projects
next Autumn as a great triumph

Into nocturnal habits
I still wait till people go to bed
before I begin

Often enough that's so
I imagine then I feel
what was there then

To anticipate is stimulus
I would desire none of this changed
nothing is of course

Though everything is different
I am curious what it might have become
the loss felt isn't personal

Choices which I don't credit though
I'm amazed at constancy
fewer and fewer

Seeing these have been kinder
I am pleased with the thought and say it is true
the thought and the pleasure

Changeable, difficult, wearing, my wife says
I am all these, you, unpredictable
uninflected stasis of grammar

•

A dummy book without language. Increasingly I secure its
temporal dimension by the use I put it to writing. Duration I
belong to, waking, sleeping, routine, memory and anticipation,
enter obliquely; it's important this takes place outside the body.
The time spent on it isn't significant, it is not trying to structure
time, I am filling this book up writing as I am able to. Every
day possibilities suggest themselves and I neglect some or omit
to enter them so the book lacks one kind of fullness which I
restore as I go along. Other things going along acquire pieces
of it those pages are no longer blank as it fills up the book
acquires passages from them. There is no palimpsest writing in
the end.

•

The telephone. In the future. I put up with the
unpleasant thinking it will be over shortly. Shortly
it's dying.

Now I'm tired, it's colder, I don't want to go to
bed yet I don't want to go on with this. I shall do
several different things in a set order and then go
to bed.

With that anticipation of future gain (or pleasure)
takes place.

It emerges much further on like spirit writing another
voice of my own to catch up.

•

Maybe that was not the weald. Driving in a different
direction the landscape was entirely familiar. Emerging
at the T-junction I knew where I should turn up hill
over the heath between the radio masts

The crossroads like schemes of time

Anticipates a jolt in someone else's lifeline
narrowly missed

All yesterday's cars
and all tomorrow's going the other way

•

The drawing you mention must be a working drawing from
a subject I used in 1963, 'The Funeral of Julian Grimau', the
Spanish marxist murdered now already ten years ago. I have
no memory of the drawing although I can picture the eventual
painting well.

•

Cars frozen into queues at petrol pumps
ignoring traffic lights
their time is not now
the signals mislead
do not stop if you intend to go

But here I can stop
with a cat asleep on my bed
only
one night away
from winding backwards
tomorrow at 6.20
the train stops
Jean gets off
I wait on the road
she climbs the stairs
passes the ticket barrier
crowds through the station doors
crosses the road diagonally
and enters my goings on
at 6.22 for both of us
I am found there
waiting for her
and here I am
setting off
to position myself
while she's alone
I mind her sleep

                                    ●

Most of that I did
believing in an attempt
at deciphering the past
out of hurried prose scribble

Timetabled days
intervene like elastic
to pull taut
and days of activity
continue unspent

trips to the municipal tip
removing broken glass, brick
slate, metal, lino
level to the foundations

Chalk

      Coke   Gas
    Electricity sneezing

Water, dripping slowly away into dust
absorbent puddle
cement
           mixture
plaster grout
nails
stick   up
hammered down

offering wounds

               •

Barked skin over the skip
heaving rubble to the back
bloody fingers
sepsis knuckles

no lint no sticking plaster

Come on
from another room
come on
beans on toast

gas fire   TV   toaster

burning

•

Now I'm about to leave again. Now I am
waiting. Now I am really leaving. Goodbye
I love you forever. Touching your cheek
Holding both hands.

Give him my love when he comes home

off in the moonlight

Ardour   ardent
            guerdon (of love)
laminate words

•

This morning

            provoked a spasm of anger
            I won't

blankfaced, ungiving
I don't understand cheery and secretive
Here is another cheery letter
Here another letter to amend for peevishness

but it is unscrutable

            that is almost perfect

Thank you for phoning

•

Silence piled in the hall
after sleep we remove
six months of closet life to undo
and spread out
between tools and materials
a box of bricks
sand, cement
a whole new weather front advances
and passes over
ice setting at once on the windscreen
fans, vaults, in two dimensions
of strength
demist spray

a see-where-it's-going
turning point
where it's about to twist
and wind back into origins
paper board cloth paste thread
the brain
magnificent frozen gel
not one odd item out

it doesn't mention this
it's all set
threads choked on life
short and ravelled
but we change for tomorrow

•

With the lees held in my mouth
rinse swallow don't spit

a new landscape this week
chalk scarp tinkered with
as far as the light bounces off
the down arched off beyond the chalkpit
not very far at all

the copper sleeves promote verdigris
the blueprint is elegant but had to be changed
the blue flare of paraffin settles down in the background
in thanks for making us warm this Christmas

the cold tank overflow drips and
                    stains over the concrete
more disposal trips all that wood
piled in the area

        Coming out
into a dark unlit street one fur coat
is very much like another whatever
was meant for your ear concerning
bed now made someone start the
embarrassment of discretion on past
midnight's extension

                            •

Someone with a sense of humour
three pints
                    rain falling
on to some hollow thing

switch off the heating
(no flue as yet) so Jean
(the right girl in my bed) and I
rise tomorrow morning
another day (later
and deeper in debt)

rubble clatters
bought but not paid for
down behind the chimney breast
past the ripped out
rotten tin baffle
and into the kitchen

asbestos board
cuts with a saw

social forces
exclusive as style
separate and waiting
corrosive substitutes

                          •

It was much more
like this

                    Hail stones
moving in its very atmospheric way
the weather changes
as we go ours up
down through and over
in metric contours

confluence of ditches
brimming waters

                    Feeding the ducks
there is never enough bread to go round
on Saturday none left in bakeries
not even stale bread

                    Then there was
Christmas I happened to make a note of the fact
here on Boxing Day

                          •

Next the question is can
they proceed beyond the opacity
of their simulacrum of analytical
language and will they be able to
confront the ontological question
if it means a redirection of their
present verbal resources?

The answer is of course No however much
we admire that pugnacity of style.

Linguistic not manual as in
'Don't come those strokes with me then.'

You can say thank you the hands
are better now

Yesterday's rigours
bricking up that hole
and cementing it over
didn't aggravate the conclusion
we have no need of finger stalls

●

Then New Year's Eve interposed its
traditional half-remembered ditties in the Bar till One
nothing modern ladies and gentlemen
in this House tonight
though the songs were this year's earlier on
fossil declarative style in
easy melody and forgotten words

Then at three o'clock I burnt my hair on the gas jet
failing to relight a cigar butt
natural gas flares
up ashen matted
tackiness flakes off

in a bed made for one two
get up the worse for rest
go back the way they entered
past the former gasworks
and over the marsh
a couple of anxious sphinxes

and then a visit and then another
and goodbye goodbye it's
not so far you know

                    •

I think you must enjoy this sudden
imposition of work at dusk
despite an inconsiderate delivery
half an hour before the lights switch off
which has to be arranged at once
on this traditional display stand

the clenched emotions line the kerb
hurrying off into shared privacy
like plastic poppers on a
quite ungraded necklet
the very order of benches on a
pay as you enter bus
stopped at traffic lights
its rigid passengers the only
illumination down the entire street
unembarrassed yet like involuntary
reflections sharing one idea
with the other candid customers

This will do and so I walk to
collect my purchase at the off-licence

Yes it is peaceful

Most peaceful last of years

                    •

That laurel that is not a bay
over there it
sways a lot

                    Why not a whole bush?

That's going to be strong
                    down there

Lightly fading home to eternity
deep blue sky and darker clouds
for a few lasting minutes before
all the lights begin to come on
and I put dinner in the oven

Tomorrow not blue
                    pink
verging on something else but then I lost it
fleeting

                    •

Rain totally insistent drizzles
as I walk downhill over the river
back across the new bridge
down by the river walk
where it smells of malt
under an arch where water rattles in
droplets on different kinds of metal
uphill once more and left down
the walled path past the meeting house
then right and up the same hill
another way step inside and out
after two pints into
pelting rain drenching for

200 yards to our house
out of my coat and shoes
sausages in fridge, oranges in bowl
where has this tin full of biscuits
come from?
reading and dozing on the couch
till the phone rings
dreaming of being awake
it's Jean at another station and
Goodness! it's Six already
a few biscuits in a paper bag
slip on my dry shoes
and twenty minutes to what
seems like an assignation
at the Bridge
a quick drink and
take her home
from work after dinner
we split a can of brown ale
and she falls asleep

●

Brought down my cart of bricks
painted doors and fanlight windows

dusted, polished, rearranged
Grandad's bright colours and now
quiet care with equal care I
rearrange each piece in its drawer
the way I remember it the
handle gone but how strange it is
painted Andrew T. K. Crozier
& Co Ltd Builders and
Contractors Phone 824
while I remember it as Knights
in yellow lettering and black dimensional
shading

                offcuts fashioned to a chip
off an old block if I rolled
a barrel of blazing tar down that
hill I'd be put away

                                              ●

But such stories persist
like something left behind just as you go through the door
not slowly perceptibly fading but suddenly
just the news of a totally new set

If turning back opened up
alternatives I assert with confidence
you would not have existed
so lacking comparison
variety is real

Revealing what there was or
it can be said to represent
what is missing

The car starts this morning without choke
the battery is dry the plates warped
gaping to be filled

No heavy duty sacks
Next there will be no polythene
Palimpsest

Find a use for these things
renew and re-use

                                              ●

Closing the attic door on memory
and bringing it down here
with me
       the miniature wagon like nothing else
but a tender (dragged behind) stands
on the floor looking old-fashioned

one cube on my shelf each
face a different colour
from a choice of six
yellow red silver gold blue black

Notes de travail   Tressell

   Saw horse   Grandfather

a table in fact a strip of asbestos
18 inches from the end of a sheet
it cuts better wet
the short saw springs from the groove

two white doors

•

Much rain the wind blew off
my cap turned Jean's umbrella
inside out

A starling flying hard past the window
beak full of bread

Ducks
uninterested at first
bread brought home for another day

Moving on not moving in
today like an extra clarity
love refracted our presences
walking down the street
into the rain still there
an after-image of complement
bodily hypnagogic we were
two but the memory is one

Asleep upstairs
the bedclothes tuck in your body heat
draughts eddy the curtains not a breath
can insinuate down your back

●

POEM OF THIS POEM

The landing light through our bedroom door
fixes your posture. I create darkness
and enter closing the door behind me
and round the bed skirting the wall
where the window faintly implies spaces
more than I feel. Undressing into the cold
with an apprehension of warmth in
regular low sounds an interval which is
continuous and repetitive as I fall
beneath the bedclothes and roll over
to my side engaging your outline and
rest. Balanced. You return to sleep
diffusing heat and moisture. The other
person I sleep with I am as ever
beside you drawn into the breaths
you take. Not speaking. Hearing such space
that slowly stills into an ambient
jointure of being. Here. Far off.
The world rises into us

●

Perched in a pear tree the starling's
puny song barely penetrates rather
it preens and fans its insignificant wing

light speckles its radiant plumage
glossily colouring where today
is dulled

The ducks aren't hungry but
sit on the island
stirring occasionally

A pair of jackdaws, or maybe rooks, but
I'm sure jackdaws appear and warm themselves
against that chimney stack
smoke on the wind winds over them
as they flex precariously against
the bricks ready now to fly
one after the other off
across the cutting

                    ●

Rarely able to sense the pregnancy of cosmos
these days I make a number of local compacts
veiled in desire for whole ground
the non-reductive
smoke from the same chimney and a garden fire
matter rising to its final state
turning along the wind and dispersing
out of sight
no image that I can grasp
more than I hope to
the fires are invisible
tightening painfully on the body to release

the heat rising towards its source
clouds mantle the world's radiance
rain falls in straight off the sea
and gleams on the pavement
inaudible creeping edge
staining each step

                              •

                    False Spring
was my muse for all this refusal of damage
as the heart rises in unlooked for sunlight
to the frantic activity of animals
within their world
behind the hedgerows

imperceptibly then it is almost over
not false but not authentic either
unlike the punctuation of night

                              •

In torchlight to know where you are
and then switch the beam off
to catch a glow at the heart of the fire
charred open at the top
but settling into itself
burning slowly to leave
scarcely any ash

flames interrupt darkness
dried out at inevitable flash point
sparks rise into the air above my head
until they extinguish no longer sparks

I am out to damp the heap down
and it's pre-dawn
                              birds all at once
cut through the air calling out

steam rises off the crying cinders
grey enough to see

but I am unused to this crispness
in the world and walk around the garden
wide awake in space

Colourless like the offering light
the world returns in primary quality
distinct as afternoon but not for me

•

Needing to wake up yet still dreaming
I return to the house where Jean waits for me sleeping

the horizon is a veil towards which I adapt
in acknowledgement of the sun
about to rise over the houses

the cool air stirs indoors and
the blinds flap at the open window
light pleating through on the floor

•

(i.m. Rolf Dieter Brinkmann)

Already the ducklings resemble their aunts and uncles
free of all obvious maternal bond
the brood moves in and out of itself
involuted and explosively bobbing
in each other's wake

their movement appears haphazard
and even elegantly natural they all
look the same and know what they want
when we appear under the shadowy leaves
with our bags of bread

it is a sign for them to
come to the edge and when it stops
and the last crumbs are shaken out
into the dirty water they move off
together again while you and I

set off round the pond talking
about ducks and the volume of foliage
on a summer branch which dips
toward the water to be reflected
in words that condense like the image

of each leaf shifting over the others
while unreflected light flickers through
in a web of shining brevity
that glows all night long
as air moves and water rises

within those immense columns
echoing : all language is truth
though a bed of dry leaves when evaporation
ceases and our words turn and fall
flickering with our life upon the earth

DUETS

FOR IAN TYSON

Punctual as returning something
now worn-out winding back
the tension in a spring
which daily use makes slack

Passed by familiar straight lines
on an array of worn-out topics
to agree to a manual of signs
at which abruptly the point sticks

Stemming back from its confluence
the topic hovers upon the air
turned inside-out in a display of patience
surrounded by ravels that hold it there

The ink flows from the cartridge
like tracer hovering in the path
it swerves across time like a bridge
to the future emptying from its bath

Level to the horizon
the jagged peaks trace beneath the star
which these telescopes imprison
like supine distance dragging on too far

Without stopping the axis turns
across the ground quite jaggedly
and goes on turning and never learns
the ground is lying flat and peacefully

Now the word quickly moves forward
tight and unrelaxed across the heart
within a confined space like Mother Hubbard
poor little dog it is time for you to part

Music perhaps this time round
heartily itself like a two-year-old
playing on its own without a sound
from what its sticky fingers hold

Bowed down by the weight of care
while in the garden on last year's buddleia
butterflies hover in the purple air
something is subsiding slowly into fear

Speak for this gentle creature
on the garden path and say its name
aloud to graft its finest feature
in your mind for you're the same

Perhaps a stroke would change it all
say for the better but maybe for the worse
an angularity from which the points fall
into dull rotundity like an empty purse

Fervent desire meshed with
sheepish sorrow but administ-
ering a commonplace come hith-
er look of imagine what you've missed

Clouds tug across the pane of blue
like sheep struggling at a gate
barred to them which they must pass through
or stay there quite abandoned to their fate

The shadow acknowledges the sun
happily in step like the body it follows
until it is swept up by clouds that run
across the sky nearly coming to blows

Not in the same place twice
unlike the well-turned rhyme
easily used unlike dice
no lightning will strike this time

A LONG STORY BUT NOT A TALL ONE

Richard Long set out to walk a line
turning it at right angles to make a square
and found it made a triangle an obvious sign
that where you start from is no longer there

Honey from onions onion round an egg
so sweetly right and latticed in the wax
of first impressions they could scarcely beg
a higher finish hanging there on racks

A spiral like a crab in the sand
washed up and dragged round in a spin
of tracks melted in the ooze and
fading out of life so brief and thin

Loosely dragged through wet snow
which rusts round the runners like nests
in a refurbished rookery all set to go
in a rush over the hill where the sun crests

Four ducks fly over a low road
running hidden by branches and the rain
they shed from their wings has slowed
to the rustle of leaves in a dry drain

Down is the same for warmth or laid
beside the head hides the longest way
round between two points quickly made
in a bed of earth to close the day

As though the air at rest is still
beaten by wings that at length have stirred
but almost hears the launching thrash and mill
of pinions streaming round the feeding bird

Such dizzy roots coil like skywriting
then stir away from the web as
emergent runners no longer short of airing
room gradually turn green beneath the gas

Now everything is upside down and insects
cast their shadows in this quarter
like light itself as it reflects
a water droplet in a drop of water

It can't be anything like sibling
likeness that has massed these lines lost in
rivalry for which one is looping
around the other like loose folds of skin

The ornaments confuse the grammar
stuffed like an aubergine and lost for
ever with a hopeless snarl of denture
polish and yet dare to ask for more

The dialectic expires on its feet
four stuffy corners superimposed
and unable to budge even to greet
the future imperfect that had never closed

Short and thin or long and curly lines
with two cast-off kinds of ending
pair off like opposites whose nature inclines
to covert types of correspondent blending

The golden section spirals growing to
be always the same two ends of crêpe
on something else a little heap of goo
within for its particular shape

Leaf tremor for a passing train
faint as a song-thrush always in the mist
in which a fox lingers like a stain
about to disappear on lips that kissed

Loopy Dupes

Fed back to the dot
in hoped-for recoil at this point
it weighs on the wound thread
of a button worn dangling
out of its normal rectitude
a test to tired memory
drawing its assent from the code book
where the dot abruptly refuses to budge
it is joined by others which trail behind
in meaningful suspension like a cloud
about to exhibit its other side waiting
for the stars to gleam through fixedly
their light oozing all the way
along the line blotted in a crease
which cuts the sky from edge
to edge like a sheet of paper
fresh from the quire its edges
deckled beneath the fingertips
which feel around such
flat expanse spread right across
the space it takes without pause
in its pointed dead-pan mimicry
of an act repeated in ignorance
over the pacified landscape surrounded
in speech which accelerates
constriction within the cardiac
vacuum of a tube half a size too large
for a pipe but the timetable
hums in its morning routine
and toddles in its valves like
a mute trumpet or a dogwhistle
from which some sweet adhesion on the lips
purses them despondently
as though a wilted border legume
festooned with royal imagos

gradually shrank under such attack
so moderate and in need of its spokesman
from the crazy paving to summon it
publicly and instil its virtues
in the unconscious collective able
maybe to metamorphose in the flesh
whether to transcend or sink
the submerged segments jumble
into the jammed coin slot of the drier
ready waiting to tangle
the shrunken garments which infest
those lower parts close to
the anticipated waking dream
snatched today by the sun
writhing through the glass
and curtains in a thermal aubade
administered to purge the passive
flanks of heliotrope saluting in
rank on rank led on by the left
to evaporate like haze that droops
overhead like tired pugilists
on a tour of remembrance
disliking the neat freeways
on which they speed between lights
at carefully adjusted mph
and maintained lane discipline
around the perimeter of the old town
which has been carefully restored
to the epoch of an imaginary childhood
of Easter eggs in foil
in closely guarded boxes
ready for desire unwrapped and
polished off while waiting
the nebulous crushed friables
cast off by the motor vortex
of deliquescence in the rubbery mud
which lifts like a facial mask

briefly hardened and fixed in plaster
caked on the eyes like copper
as it shrinks over the grease ready
to peel the orange off the sunset
before birds buzz ahead again
at steps through the wood and
their feathers fall like shadows or
coloured foliage in a drought
equally given for comfort or to
wear on a hat the furthest
choice is fully reconciled before
the grave is shovelled up
the wind dies down it seems
the nestlings have got round to flight
and listening expectantly for
streamers fanning through the party
air with someone's message
falling in a tangle on a lap
you bet like a novice out
for the day and slowly stifling
collapse eye to eye with an ankle
which hurries out of sight
its pair replacing it as
though sandwiched between mirrors
everything goes on diminishing like
itself like itself the recession is a
sultry war of imitation hanging
like a baggy suit of clothes
worn on the wrong occasion
suffused with sweat and flushed
around a desperate grimace or bare teeth
shining in the dark and demanding
an argument even on its last legs
trying to clamber into the ring
each foot in the way and speechless
to think of what it might do next
with just a mangled skin and no

loose ends of deceit weaving from
the cropped edges of such a brain
meant to side with its own like
an inflated stoppage which
grown into full mourning
for the child that uttered the man
on a specific genetic web
that quivered for a moment in the wake
of the earth as easing away it
left a predatory ghost to show
that exhalation fading from the glass.

Pretty Head

1.

Brought back to characteristic
Optimism in kept retreating go
Heavy on the coiled band
Tuned roughly speaking

2.

A line set out of plumb
On test conditions faked memory
Looks up words in the vocab
Where a finger absolutely don't point

3.

But aligns with a bunch of others
In suspense built up excess
Read to turn another over
Fixed leaves steady meant

4.

Sweated light shined all
Folded over like
Paper along a dotted line
Cover from the life

5.

A new line in consequence
Straight edged under thumb
Feel up all over that
Flat surface layered out

6.

Space filled no vacancy
Imitated to the blankness
Obsessive behaviour patterns
A captivated appeased scenery

7.

Speaks words faster
Than it tells the time
Just enough & to spare
Past a stop on schedule

8.

In the opening routines
Staggered through the morning
A funnel or a whistle
Choked on adherent lips

9.

Crease then in desperation
As if the earth skimmed
By perfect insect flight
Shrank gradually from attack

10.

Mere need a summary
Broken slab of wide awake
Admonishment to proprieties
Together in capable ignorance

11.

Different shapes of person
Either swallow or clamber over
A bloody mess of fragments mixed
In the vent hot air blocked

12.

Read to stir up
The nipped in tux the vest
These lowly neighbouring parts
Expect a dream on early call

13.

Shake out today backwards
Wiped off across the glass
The curtains heated chamber
Gags at emetic dawn

14.

Colours of blood flow
Numb on row upon row
Dry up like condense haze
Heaven like a phrase

15.

Fond memories limp
After the annual function
Vanishing ahead lights
Verge on the speed limit

16.

Compliant on the forecourt
On the periphery of old
Scrupulously rendered unto
Back in a fancy childhood

17.

Rapt with silver paper
Frugal but at their expense
Smoothed ready over
Come over weight downstairs

18.

Absorb soluble reject
Plastic insert draw out
Power dust up
Beauty put on it face

19.

Hard and to the point
Thick on the lids like brass
Greased ready to scale
Orange up to sunset

20.

Migrants quiver with distance
An echo on the silence
They moult like shadows
Watered edge of sunlight

21.

As much with comfort
As for the choice goes
Off face to face before
The tomb can be dug under

22.

The wind would seem to drop
Ere babies start their flight
Attentive listening to
The rocket of aerial calls

23.

Dressed in the message
Cut off and celebrate
Like an amateur on the loose
Day trip slow throttle

24.

Drop the sights
Drawn on your eyes
A replacement like
Squeezed between mirrors

25.

One steps forward two
Back we go dished
Out a hard identical
Shoddy off the peg

26.

Accidents spread out
Flush to chronic pink
Embarrassed empties grin
Shining exact on black

27.

But used up
Into the array
Off the words
Of what could

28.

A whole skin broke
Loose ends needed trim
Chamfer round the skull
Born again mixer

29.

Exaggerated in the way
Mourning suits it so well
The child admits to grow up
Family to private party

30.

Hesitant a moment in pursuit
The ground draws off
Leaving too its startled ghost
Condensed its image on the glass

Swoon

Consider waiting, as though not just today
but many days had made it late:
could it be the trains delayed by snow or the slow
twilight of a Victorian romance. There might be
a wall, a meeting place without a point,
the figure placed against it wearing outdoor clothes,
around it what a wall divides. But left alone
patience is visible while the fall of light persists;
the light, unbroken, has its right effect
on monumental detail no sooner has the mind
had enough of that. But how much longer
will the leaves all wear that dappled sunlight
shadows in the air. They remember nothing and invent
nothing but some choice effects
of transience and mood. See, everything
with almost the same clearness
grey twilight poured on sodden woods and grass
all things, at last, stored in myopic fullness
while the dying day is crowned with stars.

HIGH ZERO

FOR JOHN JAMES AND J. H. PRYNNE

While the grass spoils underfoot
like glass, the sound sharp and clear,
frost persists in the air while the sun rises,
looking 'as if it were a lamp of earthly flame'.

But at the surface, like a separate place
the picture of this is over-exposed. But
in shock, rare gases leave their stain to
burn its bright sign on everything.

It would flout its law: saturation by
the contents spread anecdotally (BAL).
Shored up together to breathe
you hear the brain stay tuned to you.

The evolution of the principle optic
content is an illusion. So much
like marble in sunlight. The grain
is true or stained with loss.

And for ever and a day runs on
at arm's length, held with scents
too vivid to see: beneath
the reckless apex of that hope.

A pleasure shared
            at both ends of a string
        hands oppose the work of teeth
until both unclench their grip on
condition all but nothing in the room
any longer recalls the hypotenuse
it sags and upon our feet again
hover before the onset of 'Ennui'.
                    Like angels turning our backs
                        to heed the call
of fallen comrades
                    and fall on top of them.
Shored up together to breathe
the fumes of evening
gathered in an airless room
its windows still warm to touch
are tinged with pink
reflections of faces like
stray atoms in a chaos
trying to better themselves
and liquefying painfully. The gases
rarefy towards the ceiling
heated in the light
that sets them off.

                            •

Crumpled beside yesterday
    it is a dream before birth
before the company is brought together
and the reunion commences.

Isn't this the shirt you wore?
It is time's memorial
        like a favourite colour
that no longer moves you

until you pass somebody else
in an adjacent register
and your tone noticeably changes
    in a painful seizure

    that wears you out.
Being the same size helps
but the standard remains the same
until the commencement of business

one day brings with it a complete
conversion of the measure
    everyone took for granted.
The same quantity carries forward

they claim, hopefully, new style:
    bear it in mind
for being generously impartial
you too can don the uniform.

                    •

Run into a sodden blur
of lamplight on the pavement
– as though no cracks yawned
except where children walk –
the air is heavy with mist
flat out like condensation on a window.
Surface tension vs. gravity.
It would flout its law: saturation by
an abrupt inversion of evaporation
precipitate hotness in the clammy dark.
If you can remember the sun
and make the appropriate local adjustment
its rays will fall precisely
at your feet like natural flame
to consume your thoughts.
Dry to any reflection

the burnished metal of your head
seems to repel the sunlight
by staying indoors, just before
dawn you go outside and the dew runs
from your forehead like sweat
which you wipe from your upper lip
in a conditioned reflex
action like a child.

•

The advance of happiness
is never an anniversary
nor as the evening light fades
once more and shadows disappear
into the world of objects
should one think of a return
for the light is given back
from its destination and absorbs
the atmosphere of a curtained room
within its swift recoil
and it is abruptly dark indoors
while every rambling rose gleams
like blemished skin in a cleavage
even now last night and tonight
border on resemblance
like the natural twins of an impeccable
bloodline the stock reverts
around them fruitlessly
and uniform like something gone
from memory the date not written
down and the day unobserved
for good slipping past
like thieves of time
escaping to the wilderness.

•

The stems are covered

Round them the water disappears
bluer and heavier than air
which is silvered at the surfaces
of small bubbles clustered to them

But at the surface, like a separate place
the blue is the solution
of reflected light in glass
on which repose highlights
sinking along the side of the bowl
in which the colour of the flowers
and the reflected colour of the air
wait to be wiped dry

As they're lifted out with a sponge
oil floats away from the water
in indifferent repulsion
the differentia of like from like

Out of the medium floats
the shadowed lightness of a branch
crooked with aged growth
the colours fade and harden
exposed to too much sunlight
still they adhere to the flowers
and leaves they skilfully attend.

●

All of your ideas
                    begin life again
when you wake up
        your faithful servants, already at work
        in their accustomed places
like clothes neatly folded on the chair
which no one else could wear
in quite your way, grown fat
on the success of small ambitions

which you dream about
and can't outgrow
like permanent convalescence
there's no escaping them.
The way your friends remember you
clips over like paper
cut to fit a larger model
they never seem to change
the way you do, their thoughts
were your thoughts, and they note
your points like rival connoisseurs.
Drop a coin into the slot
and a kind of truth comes out
I SPEAK YOUR MIND
one foot cheating on the ground.

●

Then in the smoke
                the extinction of light
whatever follows is masked
by tears that smart the eyes
like blurrings of hot fat:
the picture of this is over-exposed. But
from its opaque depth there emerges
a counterfeit sadness
                tender as regret, wet
as undried tears
a little smudged and reddened
a little rubbed-in message
that'll teach you. The darkness lifts
towards the horizon and stops
at the water's edge
in its deepest tone, over the rim
where all at once the sky lightens
perceptibly out of touch
like a disappearing vessel
dipping its flag conveniently,

Farewell. Whoever else
would see it quite like that
so empty just the place
to sink in out of sight.

                          •

All that it should be
                    the night long white
glow of insomnia upon glass

cloudlike as the brain where it meets
the narrow band of light clear as dust
in the eye the material world dilates

in shock, rare gases leave their stain to
register that brief catastrophe
across the stomach wall

no other aftermath
a path to the downstairs door
by way of the kitchen window

where the animals all come in
to feed in turn, nudging their plates
over the vinolay in silence

no less heavy than their sleep
and just as fugitive their days
go haunting the neighbours' gardens

animating the shadowless grass
which gleams by night in parched
neglect just covering the earth

like a tattered quilt and
patched with weeds it barely
holds the heat of the day.

                          •

In the time it takes
a beak to probe a grass's root
or a heart-beat to lose its echo
within the automatic illusion of memory
like glass, the sound sharp and clear,
too brilliant to the touch : within
the body cavity : unequal pressure
across the surfaces keeps up
the polished moment with its smears
of iridescent after-image, not quite forgotten
meals which cost too much,
a quick wipe over the formica with a damp cloth
and all's forgotten in a moment
when the breasts tilt this way
beneath her butcher's apron
adding another ten per cent
finally to level everything out
in a discreet eructation
and the instant's past again
the interrupted sounds resume
the hour in compact ratio
of undeleted silence, added
in the inventory it augments
the average of successful song.

●

Where did such sound come from
                    high heels on metal
receding over stone
          before the circuits close again
potential at the furthest ebb
gone down
          where it excludes itself.
The street dips to the left
until the lamplit haloes wane
and something follows in ensuing darkness
in the endless fading echo where

long after the machine's gone dead
you hear the brain stay tuned to you.
What would you lose?
The echo of an echo
in fugitive half-life
looped into itself until
the erasure made itself heard
over the message. Forgotten
noises clamour for attention
first thing in the morning
seeking another time zone
to transfer to before
you recollect their source.

                        •

Rain drips in the casement
                of an outdoor life
        from day to day bonheur
where condensation clings as though breath
would fly through the window
                still moving slowly
in a gathering wave at the meniscus
        ready to launch itself
in immaculate newness.
                        It ripples slowly down
the reeded glass like igniting neon
its reluctance suddenly overcome
before the air can soak it from
the surface down into the lungs
it begins to flow
directly in a current with flat
orderly movement. Beneath
the cill its cruel overflow
picked out in evidence
from the dirt where drops heavily
fell has annulled that contract.
Add your name to the glass

through which you witnessed this
time soon mists over it.

●

The cat washes audibly
and yawns at four walls
snorting and sharply rigorous
for a moment in its search
then discards like knitting
when numbers drop from
the sum no longer a true count
and everything can start over
in another place. Next door
plates of half-eaten food on the floor
wait to be cleared away
all day if you'd like the job
you have to crawl on hands and knees
to pick them up. In the sink
dried particles soak off and float
free under the surface heavy
with further saturation.
Scales dry on your fingers
next like blistered skin
they lift off like a casual symptom
you get used to overnight.
Then you can start again
keeping the animal amused for
a while back where you started.

●

Let it begin again
hopeful as a glance of recognition
at the end of a line
                    Isn't this where
frost persists in the air while the sun rises
and the light seems to dawdle
as though it was already a late morning

and the windows were opened
    the rooms airing nicely
the linen we brought tossed over the foot of the bed
in a jumble of healthy intention
If you fold the corners like this
you'll sleep more comfortably tonight
the look tired and meaningless
but the edges all straightened out
               Weren't you there
in the valley when the sun set
and the mist crept inland
like a discarded band of crêpe
the windows lighting up in ones and twos
    the rooms all taken
the luggage unpacked into drawers
most of it brand new and unmarked
if you follow metonymy.

                  •

A cloudy night
               lit from beneath
for this is earth-shine
and whatever comes between us
is permeable to our will

And see, spread in that colourless glass
the double image of the garden trees
jerks like an optical toy
you point at the sky
as though the horizon

And you are half-asleep and see less
through such an instrument than while you pointed it

The evolution of the principle optic
fibre is far from complete, we know
enough to admit as much, but

prediction is tentative. You see
intermittently through silhouettes
of trees to where across the valley
the darkness relieved along the crests
of the next hills is streaked
with falling stars.

Don't come any closer
than you are already
that's quite far enough.

·

Such feeling for symmetry is
                    in the eternal tables
where the horizon meets
the horizon in a boundary line
that surrounds us with the sky

as in a clouded retina
in which the light is like a cataract
saturated with atmosphere
until it spills with emotion
                    like a paper bag

                    covered with advertisements
which its contents render illegible because
content is an illusion. So much
that can't be looked into
in these holiday transparencies

with their lack of foreground
and focus set to infinity
as though it was a wall
                    run up by the shutter
timed to the split second

in which the sky tilts away
as the light decelerates to 0
                on a soft surface
spread for such emergencies.

                •

Another tarmac scab
under the grey lake which wrinkles:
the great skin of water
closed by the old wound of the moon.
Like a broken path to the horizon
the world is in braille
and enlarged accordingly
until its brilliance is dimmed
into the tactile surrounds
of an auditory tightrope
the yawning sea of fallen expectation
now the object is bright and opaque
like marble in sunlight. The grain
runs through the mountain to emerge
running at its foot in the surf
which foams in fragments heaped up
like beds of rubble. Halfway along
only the air is visible
and frightful, not half fast enough
for anything but a low-pitched green
blur no further off
than it looks. Black out
in either direction
and fall like Icarus.

                •

Light is in the curtains
like a bright veil of numbers
that rises in folds over and over
and the calculus of persistence
undogmatic and fluent in its changes
draws back with the weave
its light released

in a white rinse.
                        Shaken out
like sparks from a bed of embers
dimmer and dimmer to the touch
but there to be drawn back
the shadows fall into the room.

And for ever and a day runs on
without resistance, turned
to a dead stop without a shudder
and starting again without pause
the world takes it all back
reversed.
                Overhead the gears seemed
for ever about to slip
under the strain they bore
but the tension was maintained
in all that measured track of time.

                        ●

It is
the one after
                becomes
        an accomplishment
not refused

        it is expected
your turn   will come
                        if

late still
you thought

                this time
                can be
        understood
            another rung
            of the sublime

too vivid to see: beneath
                    is less
            and far from
                    underfoot
the skin

is the margin
        which decides
            you
    from now on.

•

Stones, leaves, broken blossoms
drift from all the seasons
here beneath the misty bushes
all laid up as if winter
was anything but a time of separation
within the edges of an all–over sky
which shrinks down to the horizon
and rather a rich hoard of unreluctant
souvenirs of other weathers
from which to select a fragment
your happiness needs just such a moment
to disclose the earth as if a cloud
is true or stained with loss.
Dew creeps along the filaments
towards the gathering centre
and unable to support itself
at last falls from the web
like recorded sound to fill
a place in the archive, spreading
its softening touch beneath
everything else, down to the root
of the matter like an axiom
that's always so reliable
there's a cue to use it.

•

The scenario of lies
dresses up to kill
and the leaves drift into heaps
while the grass spoils underfoot
like last year's snow
in congealed pellets of green mud
honestly you wipe your feet
on the guest mat and feel 'Welcome'
ascend through the leather like an
artful ray of hope. Oh no
the contents spread anecdotally (BAL)
and cure you of all that, what?
It just wants discipline O'Grady says.
Done with all that pass on
down the line of withered plants
and take a leaf from every other one
they're overdosed with Paris green
past any joke. Even the blue
is hard to pin a name to
preferring to describe an empty
sky in French. Sublime.
The air is choked with metal
and looks like watered silk
rolled out over heaven.

•

There they were surrounded
        by their infidelities
waiting to be catalogued and indexed
in the list of recurrent solutions
to problems of the modern world
some for the fourth and fifth times.

Afterwards they return home
some on buses, others by train
or car and go to bed by
twelve and at once turn off the light

to dream in innocence, the keys
to their fear among the small change
and other bits and pieces emptied
from their pockets like guilt.

Their nudity is a dirty joke
the reckless apex of that hope.

They dream of noble landscapes
and a savage truth and get
up dressed and ready to kill
for what they believe in
spite, the generous talk, of
consciousness raised like a
speculative loan
they ask for more than they can give.

●

Expensive dried flowers beside
your eyes in a mirror
smooth wet and dry in one light
of present accommodation
looking 'as if it were a lamp of earthly flame'.
The unfaded everlastings
and the lustre of your irises
hardly resemble one another
do they? The light expires
and with its waning flames
the metered stars go out
like flowers wrenched from the stalk.
Petals litter the carpet
and weave into the design
the hazard of their immaculate lives
settled in the dust
like ungathered nectar. The pupil
flickers in the morning light
like a black insect

dancing towards the sun
in a pattern of flowers.
The colours swarm abundantly
each has its specialist
and I am yours.

                    •

Under the umbrella
        of invisible starlight at noon
all the plants come out
        of shelter like new things
but each has a name
        given for the occasion
the visible thing it is
        a naked chance for speech
to flirt in the shrubbery
        reading all the nameplates
aromatically, by sinister touch
        a perfect stranger's sense
of decorum when abroad
        keeping the railings on the right
at arm's length, held with scents
        not straying from the path
and keeping off the grass
        which needs no label
for its name is lawn
        opening among the trees
to let the light down
        to the lowest green thing
which colours gratefully
        all that it surrounds.

                    •

Yes that's very good
                more beautiful
and no less true
        than ever before.
                Say it again.

You cannot say it again.
Burn its bright sign on everything
it sheds a
                pallor on the afternoon
as colour disappears under the highlights
in these prints.
                        This time last year
was no different
the swifts will home to their nests
like bees to the scabious
beautiful in their kind
the way we remember them.
But beyond recall
for such places to recur
the colours must each revive
in their very locations
rhyming the whole spectrum
in a retained sequence
beginning nowhere.

Begin life again
from day to day bonheur
snorting and sharply rigorous

at the end of a line
let it begin again
it is a dream before birth

The advance of happiness

UTAMARO VARIATIONS

The colours break out and float
In the appearance of a world
Reflecting the shadows of a boat

As though an inner life unfurled
Like waves and eddying water
In a photograph its edges curled

With age while life still shorter
Yet fluent to its briefest detail
Traces its surface through another quarter

The way it passes covered without fail
Where underneath the sea in one deep note
Falls from the horizon like a veil

●

Dust coats the leaves with a sultry pallor
Impervious to shadow though shadow
Falls across a field empty of colour

Like a grid crumpled into shallow
Folds or in an unploughed field breaks
Up in the stubble like yellow

Light spread in a ragged sheet and takes
More of the earth than it does of air
Which stiff with glare and distance makes

The far-off hills seem near the bare
Chalk in the cutting meets their fuller
Slope to slide beneath the eyes' unshaded stare

●

     Beneath the surface
     Of clear and broken
     Colours waves like lace

     Fade in unwoken
     Substance after all
     Nothing has spoken

     Forth from the wet pall
     That skirts round at eye
     Level like a wall

     Built along the sky
     Until empty space
     Breaks where seagulls cry

●

The sun breaks through the leaves
In a spectral flare and edges
Their turning colours with fringed sleeves

Of smoke risen through clear ledges
In sunlight where greys seem to catch
A shape and substance it alleges

Are contained invisibly in each patch
Of shadow flickering among beams
Along the ground unable to detach

Its clearer outline from a tone which gleams
Beneath so thickened that if light deceives
Smoke ravelling a margin is what it seems

Driftwood and Seacoal

These men are on their feet, not all day long, when they may be on their knees or sitting on their backsides for all I know, but characteristically and most visibly they are upright, resting or in slow motion, entire and self-contained in their activity, relentlessly static. They have overcoats and caps, and the set of their heads to their shoulders, an inflexible terseness about the neck, recurring in the way the cap flattens and spreads the skull, and the overcoat's abrupt hem straightens across a stiffness behind the knee, wraps them in mistaken identity, never close enough to make apology necessary. There is something rigid between the collar bones and the scalp, between the way the knot of the tie lies against the throat and the forehead disappears beneath the headband, as though the regularity of the features is worn like an alibi. I am not where you place me. I am going down the road leading from the council estate, I am standing on the foreshore, but who you took me for must, you now realise, be miles away from where you thought you just recognised him.

What forgiveness in renewal of such error! You return as them. Stopped short again, face to face with your type, squared off from his surroundings in which I was a passer-by, I keep forgetting that you can't be here. Forgetting the vagrancy of the moment, the distances and waiting, whatever was expected, as his figure approaches, rather flat, the weight carried down the length of the spine, short legs holding the ground beneath their feet, I am out of this place, pulled together in the passage of time. Old enough, these men must be, as if belonging anywhere was now a pointless question. Why, still there of course, as long as I can remember, looking in front of them, they're like this, wherever you are. Their memories are longer still, it shows in the hang of the coat, like a box to put things in, and the low heels of tightly knotted shoes. Years of another life, of weather in the streets and the air indoors, the hours of work, the regularity of habits, when all choices are the same, the cut of the coat, the peak of the cap, and the colour of the shoes, the size in collars, the taste in ties, the pullover and braces, determined footsteps of a steady descent, bearing it all back.

I see the difference in them, collecting from the confused after-image of wishful thinking, their presence diminished to the daily scale, going about some known business. Out for a walk will do, in these surroundings, not calling for a nod of even passing acknowledgment: people live round here. They look the same. They look out against the same earth or sea or sky, the most incommunicative of languages, speechless theatres of space, the machinery of gods. No answering back, no resonant echo, but speak for yourself. Your early history is legend, the fit of your build, the gait from the past, O never-forgotten! Those massed identities, spread one way and another, banked and scattered in new neighbourhoods. I hold them like your bearing in me, between a beacon and the showy stars, looking along the pebbles on the beach. So others in us, if, not therefore not, but also, go separately together.

The Heifer

after Carl Rakosi

From the river bank she saw the fields
with ditches round them full of water.

"The mist had gone. Where were we?"

Striped woollen dress
all morning made our order breakfast
still hungry for more toast and coffee.
The tea-urns bubbled in a corner.
We were together on stools and benches,
at snack-bar counters near the window,
in bars soon after they were open.

"Tell me. Where were we?"

We were inside
both our pasts
and our future
where our paths crossed
                    in a crowded hallway
and the gas-fire of a furnished room
and an early fenland autumn
                    are our memory,

where the light hardened
                  into a shape
and in all directions
                  earth and sky met.

We were where we have not lost
each other's separate power
as if at once
to see together . . .
the simple tenderness
of a heifer licking a post,
forever lost . . .

                    forever to be lost.

Donald Davie

SELECTED
POEMS

Contents

At Knaresborough

'Broad acres, sir.' You hear them in my talk.
As tell-tale as a pigment in the skin,
Vowels as broad as all the plain of York
Proclaim me of this country and your kin.

And, gratified to have your guess endorsed,
You warm to me. I thaw, and am approved.
But, to be frank, the sentiment is forced
When I pretend, for your sake, to be moved.

To feel so little, when his sympathies
Would be so much engaged (he would have said),
Surprised the poet too. But there it is,
The heart is not to be solicited.

Believe me, sir, I only ply my trade,
Which is to know when I am played upon.
You might have moved, you never shall persuade.
You grow too warm. I must be moving on.

Zip!

I'd have the silence like a heavy chock
That's kicked away as you begin to read;
And sense, responding to the tiny shock,
Roll forward, fire, and smoothly gather speed.

Lines should be hoops that, vibrantly at rest,
Devolve like cables as the switches trip,
Each syllable entailing all the rest,
And rhymes that strike, exploding like a whip.

I'd have the spark that leaps upon the gun
By one short fuse, electrically clear;
And all be done before you've well begun.
(It is reverberations that you hear.)

Eight Years After

If distance lends enchantment to the view,
Enormities should not be scrutinised.
What's true of white, holds of black magic too;
And, indistinct, evil is emphasised.

Gilfillan, telling how the poet Churchill
'Indulged in nameless orgies', makes us smile;
We think such large unutterables fill
Vapid lacunæ in a frowzy style.

A case however can be made for this:
The queasy Levite need not be ashamed
To have no stomach for atrocities.
We brook them better, once they have been named.

For fearsome issues, being squarely faced,
Grow fearsomely familiar. To name
Is to acknowledge. To acquire the taste
Comes on the heels of honouring the claim.

'Let nothing human be outside my range.'
Yet horrors named make exorcisms fail:
A thought once entertained is never strange,
But who forgets the face 'beyond the pale'?

Remembering the 'Thirties

I

Hearing one saga, we enact the next.
We please our elders when we sit enthralled;
But then they're puzzled; and at last they're vexed
To have their youth so avidly recalled.

It dawns upon the veterans after all
That what for them were agonies, for us
Are high-brow thrillers, though historical;
And all their feats quite strictly fabulous.

This novel written fifteen years ago,
Set in my boyhood and my boyhood home,
These poems about 'abandoned workings', show
Worlds more remote than Ithaca or Rome.

The Anschluss, Guernica – all the names
At which those poets thrilled or were afraid
For me mean schools and schoolmasters and games;
And in the process some-one is betrayed.

Ourselves perhaps. The Devil for a joke
Might carve his own initials on our desk,
And yet we'd miss the point because he spoke
An idiom too dated, Audenesque.

Ralegh's Guiana also killed his son.
A pretty pickle if we came to see
The tallest story really packed a gun,
The Telemachiad an Odyssey.

II

Even to them the tales were not so true
As not to be ridiculous as well;
The ironmaster met his Waterloo,
But Rider Haggard rode along the fell.

'Leave for Cape Wrath tonight!' They lounged away
On Fleming's trek or Isherwood's ascent.
England expected every man that day
To show his motives were ambivalent.

They played the fool, not to appear as fools
In time's long glass. A deprecating air
Disarmed, they thought, the jeers of later schools;
Yet irony itself is doctrinaire,

And, curiously, nothing now betrays
Their type to time's derision like this coy
Insistence on the quizzical, their craze
For showing Hector was a mother's boy.

A neutral tone is nowadays preferred.
And yet it may be better, if we must,
To praise a stance impressive and absurd
Than not to see the hero for the dust.

For courage is the vegetable king,
The sprig of all ontologies, the weed
That beards the slag-heap with his hectoring,
Whose green adventure is to run to seed.

Time Passing, Beloved

Time passing, and the memories of love
Coming back to me, carissima, no more mockingly
Than ever before; time passing, unslackening,
Unhastening, steadily; and no more
Bitterly, beloved, the memories of love
Coming into the shore.

How will it end? Time passing and our passages of love
As ever, beloved, blind
As ever before; time binding, unbinding
About us; and yet to remember
Never less chastening, nor the flame of love
Less like an ember.

What will become of us? Time
Passing, beloved, and we in a sealed
Assurance unassailed
By memory. How can it end,
This siege of a shore that no misgivings have steeled,
No doubts defend?

Dream Forest

These have I set up,
Types of ideal virtue,
To be authenticated
By no one's Life and Times,
But by a sculptor's logic

Of whom I have commanded,
To dignify my groves,
Busts in the antique manner,
Each in the space mown down
Under its own sway:

First, or to break the circle,
Brutus, imperious, curbed
Not much by the general will,
But by a will to be curbed,
A preference for limits;

Pushkin next, protean
Who recognised no checks
Yet brooked them all – a mind
Molten and thereby fluent,
Unforced, easily strict;

The next, less fortunate,
Went honourably mad,
The angry annalist
Of hearth and marriage bed,
Strindberg – a staring head.

Classic, romantic, realist,
These have I set up.
These have I set, and a few trees.
When will a grove grow over
This mile upon mile of moor?

A Winter Talent

Lighting a spill late in the afternoon,
I am that coal whose heat it should unfix;
Winter is come again, and none too soon
For meditation on its raft of sticks.

Some quick bright talents can dispense with coals
And burn their boats continually, command
An unreflecting brightness that unrolls
Out of whatever firings come to hand.

What though less sunny spirits never turn
The dry detritus of an August hill
To dangerous glory? Better still to burn
Upon that gloom where all have felt a chill.

Heigh-ho on a Winter Afternoon

There is a heigh-ho in these glowing coals
By which I sit wrapped in my overcoat
As if for a portrait by Whistler. And there is
A heigh-ho in the bird that noiselessly
Flew just now past my window, to alight
On winter's moulding, snow; and an alas,
A heigh-ho and a desultory chip,
Chip, chip on stone from somewhere down below.

Yes I have 'mellowed', as you said I would,
And that's a heigh-ho too for any man;
Heigh-ho that means we fall short of alas
Which sprigs the grave of higher hopes than ours.
Yet heigh-ho too has its own luxuries,
And salts with courage to be jocular
Disreputable sweets of wistfulness,
By deprecation made presentable.

What should we do to rate the long alas
But skeeter down a steeper gradient?
And then some falls are still more fortunate,
The meteors spent, the tragic heroes stunned
Who go out like a light. But here the chip,
Chip, chip will flake the stone by slow degrees,
For hour on hour the fire will gutter down,
The bird will call at longer intervals.

North Dublin

St George's, Hardwicke Street,
Is charming in the Church of Ireland fashion:
The best of Geneva, the best of Lambeth
Aesthetically speaking
In its sumptuously sober
Interior, meet.

A continuous gallery, clear glass in the windows,
An elegant conventicle
In the Ionian order –
What dissenter with taste
But would turn, on these terms
Episcopalian?

'Dissenter' and 'tasteful' are contradictions
In terms, perhaps, and my fathers
Would ride again to the Boyne
Or with scythes to Sedgemoor, or splinter
The charming fanlights in this charming slum
By their lights, rightly.

The Fountain

Feathers up fast, and steeples; then in clods
Thuds into its first basin; thence as surf
Smokes up and hangs; irregularly slops
Into its second, tattered like a shawl;
There, chill as rain, stipples a danker green,
Where urgent tritons lob their heavy jets.

For Berkeley this was human thought, that mounts
From bland assumptions to inquiring skies,
There glints with wit, fumes into fancies, plays
With its negations, and at last descends,
As by a law of nature, to its bowl
Of thus enlightened but still common sense.

We who have no such confidence must gaze
With all the more affection on these forms,
These spires, these plumes, these calm reflections, these
Similitudes of surf and turf and shawl,
Graceful returns upon acceptances.
We ask of fountains only that they play,

Though that was not what Berkeley meant at all.

With the Grain

I

Why, by an ingrained habit, elevate
    Into their own ideas
Activities like carpentry, become
    The metaphors of graining?
Gardening, the one word, tilth? Or thought,
    The idea of having ideas,
Resolved into images of tilth and graining?

An ingrained habit . . . This is fanciful:
    And there's the rub
Bristling, where the irritable block
    Screams underneath the blade
Of love's demand, or in crimped and gouged-out
    Shavings only, looses
Under a peeling logic its perceptions.

Language (mine, when wounding,
    Yours, back-biting) lacks
No whorl nor one-way shelving. It resists,
    Screams its remonstrance, planes
Reluctantly to a level. And the most
    Reasonable of settlements betrays
Unsmoothed resentment under the caress.

II

The purest hue, let only the light be sufficient
    Turns colour. And I was told
If painters frequent St Ives
    It is because the light
There, under the cliff, is merciful. I dream
    Of an equable light upon words
And as painters paint in St Ives, the poets speaking.

Under that cliff we should say, my dear,
    Not what we mean, but what
The words would mean. We should speak,
    As carpenters work,
With the grain of our words. We should utter
    Unceasingly the hue of love
Safe from the battery of changeable light.

(Love, a condition of such fixed colour,
    Cornwall indeed, or Wales
Might foster. Lovers in mauve,
    Like white-robed Druids
Or the Bards in blue, would need
    A magical philtre, no less,
Like Iseult's, to change partners.)

III

Such a fourth estate of the realm,
    Hieratic unwinking
Mauve or blue under skies steel-silver,
    Would chamfer away
A knot in the grain of a streaming light, the glitter
    Off lances' points, that moved
A sluggish Froissart to aesthetic feeling.

And will the poet, carpenter of light,
    Work with the grain henceforward?
If glitterings won't fetch him
    Nor the refractory crystal,
Will he never again look into the source of light
    Aquiline, but fly
Always out of the sun, unseen till softly alighting?

Why, by an ingrained habit, elevate
       Into the light of ideas
The colourful trades, if not like Icarus
       To climb the beam? High lights
Are always white, but this ideal sun
       Dyes only more intensely, and we find
Enough cross-graining in the most abstract nature.

For an Age of Plastics

With the effect almost of carving the hillside
    They climb in their stiff terraces, these houses
Feed the returning eye with national pride
    In the 'built to last'. Approving elegance
Where there is only decency, the eye
    Applauds the air of nothing left to chance
Or brilliantly provisional. Not the fact
    But the air of it, the illusion, we observe;
Chance in the bomb sight kept these streets intact
    And razed whole districts. Nor was the lesson lost
On the rebuilt Plymouth, how an age of chance
    Is an age of plastics. In a style pre-cast
Pre-fabricated, and as if its site
    Were the canyon's lip, it rises out of rubble
Sketchily massive, moulded in bakelite.

Annoyed to take a gloomy sort of pride
    In numbering our losses, I suppose
The ploughman ceased his carving of the hillside
    And all the coulters and the chisels broke
When he was young whom we come home to bury,
    A man like clay in the hands of his womenfolk.

A ploughman carved three harvests, each a son,
    Upon the flesh of Wales. And all were carried
Long since from those hillsides, yet this one
    Comes first to threshing. Nutriment and grain
For all the mashing of the interim
    Live in the load of him. Living again
His shipwright's years, the countryman's walks in the park,
    The scrape of a mattock in a too small garden,
The marriage to the capable matriarch,
    What would he change? Perhaps a stubbornness
That bristled sometimes, for the sensible hands
    To circumvent and gentle, would be less

Amenable to their shaping. But all told,
   His edged tools still would lie in the garden shed,
Still he would flow, himself, from mould to mould.

Whatever he showed of something in the rough,
   Sluggish in flow and unadaptable,
I liked him for; affecting to be gruff,
   An awkward customer – so much was due,
He seemed to think, to what a man was, once:
   Something to build with, take a chisel to.

Wide France

Sunlight so blurred with clouds we couldn't tell
Light from shade, driving to Vézelay
Disgusted you that Northern day. You thought
Caressing weather started at Calais,

And I had thought, in Burgundy; and still,
When we had stolen guiltily from where
Mummy lay wretched in the loud hotel,
All we found was squall-dashed street and square.

Nothing to do but go to Vézelay
That afternoon. Both worried, and the seasons
Wrong as usual, winter in our bones,
We drove the ten miles for the worst of reasons.

Let me remind you. First there was a strong
High, famous church; and where the hillside falls
Away behind it, France was spread at our feet;
And at our back old streets and gates and walls.

Poor eight-year-old, but how could you remember?
So many, before and since; and such a fuss
As we always made, as if to convince ourselves.
And now you worry about the eleven-plus.

Barnsley Cricket Club

Now the heat comes, I am demoralised.
Important letters lie unanswered, dry
Shreds of tobacco spike the typewriter,
No undertaking but is ill-advised.

Unanswerable even the shortest missive,
Replies not sealed, or sealed without conviction.
Thumb-marks dry out, leaving the paper pouchy,
Tousled with effort, desperate, inconclusive.

'A thing worth doing is worth doing well,'
Says Shaw Lane Cricket Ground
Between the showers of a July evening,
As the catch is held and staid hand-clappings swell.

This almost vertical sun, this blur of heat,
All stinging furze and snagged unravelling,
Denies the axiom which has kept
My father's summers shadowy and sweet.

Remembering many times when he has laughed
Softly, and slapped his thigh, because the trap
So suavely set was consummately sprung,
I wish, to all I love, his love of craft.

Hard to instruct myself, and then my son,
That things which would be natural are done
After a style less consummate; that an art's
More noble office is to leave half-done.

How soon the shadows fall, how soon and long!
The score-board stretches to a grandson's feet.
This layabout July in another climate
Ought not to prove firm turf, well-tended, wrong.

The Cypress Avenue

My companion kept exclaiming
At fugitive aromas;
She was making a happy fuss
Of flower-naming.

And I, who had taken her there . . .
Not one scent could I name
In the resinous die-straight avenue's
Plume-irrigated air.

Her world was properly indexed:
The names were in my head
Familiar, double-columned, but
Hardly a page of text.

Just the swaying channel of shade;
The stippling everywhere
Of an otherwise dust-choked country;
The difference cypress made.

*   *   *

That night at the family sing-song
She had no repertoire;
Her ear was a true one, though
Her voice not very strong.

And that was an index too!
Hymns, shanties, popular numbers,
Ballads, rounds – how many
It turned out that we knew!

And what an encyclopaedia
Of smudged ill-printed feeling
They opened up, although to
Only a coarsened ear.

A Christening

What we do best is breed:
August Bank Holiday, whole
Populations explode

Across the wolds and in a slot
Of small cars pullulate
By couples. Millington Meadows

Flower with campstools. At
Beverley the font
Has a cover carved like a goblet.

The new baby is fed.
I stumble back to bed.
I hear the owls for a long time

Hunting. Or are they never
In the winter grey of before dawn,
Those pure long quavers,

Cries of love? I put my arms around you.
Small mice freeze among tussocks.
The baby wails in the next room.

Upstairs Mrs Ramsden
Dies, and the house
Is full of the cries of the newborn.

In red and smoky wood
A follower of Wren
Carved it at Beverley:

The generous womb that drops
Into the sanctified water immediate fruit.
What we do best is breed.

A Lily at Noon

Deep-sea frost, and
Lilies at noon . . .
Late leaves, late leaves
Toss every day.
The daymoon shines always for some.
In the marriage of a slow man
Eighteen years is soon.

Sun and moon, no
Dark between,
Foresight and hindsight
Halving the hours.
And now he collects his thoughts
Before it is too late.
But what can 'too late' mean?

Shielding with hands,
Binding to stakes . . .
Late leaves, late leaves
Toss every day,
The sun moves on from noon.
To freeze, to cup, to retard –
These measures terror takes.

Rodez

Northward I came, and knocked in the coated wall
At the door of a low inn scaled like a urinal
With greenish tiles. The door gave, and I came

Home to the stone north, every wynd and snicket
Known to me wherever the flattened cat
Squirmed home to a hole between housewall and paving.

Known! And in the turns of it, no welcome,
No flattery of the beckoned lighted eye
From a Rose of the rose-brick alleys of Toulouse.

Those more than tinsel garlands, more than masks,
Unfading wreaths of ancient summers, I
Sternly cast off. A stern eye is the graceless

Bulk and bruise that at the steep uphill
Confronts me with its drained-of-colour sandstone
Implacably. The Church. It is Good Friday.

Goodbye to the Middle Ages! Although some
Think that I enter them, those centuries
Of monkish superstition, here I leave them

With their true garlands, and their honest masks,
Every fresh flower cast on the porch and trodden,
Raked by the wind at the Church door on this Friday.

Goodbye to all the centuries. There is
No home in them, much as the dip and turn
Of an honest alley charmingly deceive us.

And yet not quite goodbye. Instead almost
Welcome, I said. Bleak equal centuries
Crowded the porch to be deflowered, crowned.

July, 1964

I smell a smell of death.
Roethke, who died last year
with whom I drank in London,
wrote the book I am reading;
a friend, of a firm mind,
has died or is dying now,
a telegram informs me;
the wife of a neighbour died
in three quick months of cancer.

Love and art I practise;
they seem to be worth no more
and no less than they were.
The firm mind practised neither.
It practised charity
vocationally and
yet for the most part truly.
Roethke, who practised both,
was slack in his art by the end.

The practice of an art
is to convert all terms
into the terms of art.
By the end of the third stanza
death is a smell no longer;
it is a problem of style.
A man who ought to know me
wrote in a review
my emotional life was meagre.

A Meeting of Cultures

Iced with a vanilla
Of dead white stone, the Palace
Of Culture is a joke

Or better, a vast villa
In some unimaginable suburb
Of Perm or Minsk.

Ears wave and waggle
Over the poignant Vistula,
Horns of a papery stone.

Not a wedding-cake but its doily!
The Palace of Culture sacks
The centre, the dead centre

Of Europe's centre, Warsaw.
The old town,
Rebuilt, is a clockwork toy.

I walked abroad in it,
Charmed and waylaid
By a nursery joy:

Hansel's and Gretel's city!
Their house of gingerbread
That lately in

Horrific forest glooms
Of Germany
Bared its ferocity

Anew, resumes its gilt
For rocking-horse rooms
In Polish rococo.

Diseased imaginations
Extant in Warsaw's stone
Her air makes sanative.

How could a D.S.O.
Of the desert battles live,
If it were otherwise,

In his wooden cabin
In a country wood
In the heart of Warsaw

As the colonel did, who for
The sake of England took
Pains to be welcoming?

More jokes then. And the wasps humming
Into his lady's jam
That we ate with a spoon

Out in the long grass. Shades,
Russian shades out of old slow novels,
Lengthened the afternoon.

The North Sea

North Sea, Protestant sea,
I have come to live on your shore
In the low countries of England.
    A shallow gulf north-westward
Into the Isle of Ely
And the Soke of Peterborough
Is one long arm of the cold vexed sea of the North.

Having come to this point, I dare say
That every sea of the world
Has its own ambient meaning:
The Mediterranean, archaic, pagan;
The South Atlantic, the Roman Catholic sea.

But somewhere in mid-America
All of this grows tiresome,
The needles waver and point wildly

And then they settle and point
Somewhere on the ridge of the Andes
And the Rocky Mountains
True to the end of the world.

Pacific is the end of the world,
Pacific, peaceful.

And I do not know whether to fear
More in myself my bent to that end or
The vast polyp rising and beckoning,
Christ, grey-green, deep in the sea off Friesland.

January

Arable acres heave
Mud and a few bare trees
Behind St Michael's
Kirby le Soken, where
The pew I share
Promises the vicinity I leave.

Diatribe and
Denunciation, where
I spend my days,
Populous townships, sink
Into the haze that lowers
Over my neighbour's land.

Resignation, oh winter tree
At peace, at peace . . .
Read it what way you will,
A wish that fathers. In a field between
The Sokens, Thorpe and Kirby, stands
A bare Epiphany.

A Winter Landscape near Ely

It is not life being short,
Death certain, that is making
Those faintly coffee-coloured
Gridiron marks on the snow
Or that row of trees heart-breaking.

What stirs us when a curtain
Of ice-hail dashes the window?
It is the wasteness of space
That a man drives wagons into
Or plants his windbreak in.

Spaces stop time from hurting.
Over verst on verst of Russia
Are lime-tree avenues.

Epistle. To Enrique Caracciolo Trejo

(Essex)

A shrunken world
Stares from my pages.
What a pellet the authentic is!
My world of poetry,
Enrique, is not large.
Day by day it is smaller.
These poems that you have
Given me, I might
Have made them English once.
Now they are inessential.
The English that I feel in
Fears the inauthentic
Which invades it on all sides
Mortally. The style may die of it,
Die of the fear of it,
Confounding authenticity with essence.

Death, an authentic subject,
Jaime Sabinès has
Dressed with the yew-trees of funereal trope.
It cannot be his fault
If the English that I feel in
Feels itself too poor
Spirited to plant a single cypress.
It is afraid of showing, at the grave-side,
Its incapacity to venerate
Life, or the going of it. These are deaths,
These qualms and horrors shade the ancestral ground.

Sabinès in another
Poem comes down
To the sound of pigeons on a neighbour's tiles,
A manifest of gladness.
Such a descent on clapping wings the English
Contrives to trust
No longer. My own garden
Crawls with a kind of obese
Pigeon from Belgium; they burst through cracking branches
Like frigate-birds.

Still in infested gardens
The year goes round,
A smiling landscape greets returning Spring.
To see what can be said for it, on what
Secure if shallow ground
Of feeling England stands
Unshaken for
Her measure to be taken
Has taken four bad years
Of my life here. And now
I know the ground:
Humiliation, corporate and private,
Not chastens but chastises
This English and this verse.

I cannot abide the new
Absurdities day by day,
The new adulterations.
I relish your condition,
Expatriate! though it be among
A people whose constricted idiom
Cannot embrace the poets you thought to bring them.

Sunburst

The light wheels and comes in
over the seawall
and the bitten turf
that not only wind has scathed but
all this wheeling and flashing, this
sunburst comes across us.

At Holland on Sea
at an angle from here and
some miles distant
a fisherman reels back blinded,
a walker is sliced in two.
The silver disc came at them
edgewise, seconds ago.

Light that robes us, does it?
Limply, as robes do, moulded
to the frame of Nature? It
has no furious virtue?

A Death in the West

May's, whose mouth was
Open under the gauze.
She lay like a child in her coffin.
Often in that front parlour,
Excessively peremptory,
She struggled to belie
Her timorous nature.

Her sisters found the funds
She lacked, of confidence
To train her for a trade.
Her profession was children's nurse.
Children of conspicuous parents
Grew up under her care
To figure in divorce-scandals.

She and her sister sat
Plumb on grey sands in Cornwall
One day, the two most planted
And stubborn tubs in Nature.
Vivid in pastel sweaters,
We walked along by the cliffs
Over the eye-bright shingle.

She deluded us after all.
If she could not be forceful,
Could she be stolid? She
Liked to sit on the sands,
Looking at wide wet beaches,
Scud over Cornish seas, and
Bright shirts under the cliff.

If one of her ancient charges
Had come in a beach-wrap, stalking,
His tired eyes fierce with gin
From foreign embassies,
Her eyes had been equipped
By so much seaside watching
To know him for Ulysses.

From the New World

for Paul Russell–Gebbett

Old Glory at halfmast
For Adlai Stevenson
Drooped under PepsiCola
Flashing all night on Lima.

There, smiling and contained
And lawless through
The boardrooms of New Spain
Don Felix passed;

Smiling and contained
And lawless through
The boardrooms of New Spain,
He ushered us, and was

One of us. His son
Is at Downside,
His English flawless and
His manners too.

British is what we are.
Once an imperial nation,
Our hands are clean now, empty.
Cause for congratulation.

Plaintive the airs
With sorrows when, sails set
Against miscegenation,
Our keels leaned in from Europe.

Freight of Atlantic airs
When doxies lined the rail;
Songs of the Cavaliers
Twanged on the tainted gales;

The English fever-ships,
Though hopes re-painted, fetched
Up on the Carolinas
To wailing strings.

Rubber-faced Uncle Sam!
Unhappy Adlai,
Dipping in on the clipper to
The heritable blame,

The melancholy strains
No one alive has lived with:
England's historic guilt,
France's, or Spain's.

'What', said our diplomat,
'Sort of nation is
This that I represent
In South America?' I said:

'A nation of theatre-people,
Purveyors, not creators,
Adaptable cyphers, stylists,
Educators, dandies.'

Rubber-faced Uncle Sam!
Unhappy Adlai,
A name that is of Zion . . .
British is what I am.

Zion, a park in Utah.
So many available styles!
Heavens, the New is New
Still, to us quizzical monsters!

Barnsley, 1966

Wind-claps of soot and snow
Beat on the Railway Hotel's
Tall round-headed window;
I envy loquacious Wales.

Taciturn is the toast
Hereabouts. Were this Wales,
My father had ruled this roost,
Word-spinner, teller of tales.

If he missed his niche
I am glad of it today.
I should not have liked him rich,
Post-prandial, confident, bawdy.

He was rinsed with this town's dirt
For seventy wind-whipped years,
Chapped lips smiling at hurt,
Eyes running with dirty tears.

Or, Solitude

A farm boy lost in the snow
Rides his good horse, Madrone,
Through Iowan snows for ever
And is called 'alone'.

Because gone from the land
Are the boys who knew it best
Or best expressed it, gone
To Boston or Out West,

And the breed of the horse Madrone,
With its bronco strain, is strange
To the broken sod of Iowa
That used to be its range,

The metaphysicality
Of poetry, how I need it!
And yet it was for years
What I refused to credit.

To a Brother in the Mystery

Circa 1290

The world of God has turned its two stone faces
One my way, one yours. Yet we change places
A little, slowly. After we had halved
The work between us, those grotesques I carved
There in the first bays clockwise from the door,
That was such work as I got credit for
At York and Beverley: thorn-leaves twined and bent
To frame some small and human incident
Domestic or of venery. Each time I crossed
Since then, however, underneath the vast
Span of our Mansfield limestone, to appraise
How you cut stone, my emulous hard gaze
Has got to know you as I know the stone
Where none but chisels talk for us. I have grown
Of my own way of thinking yet of yours,
Seeing your leafage burgeon there by the doors
With a light that, flickering, trenches the voussoir's line;
Learning your pre-harmonies, design
Nourished by exuberance, and fine-drawn
Severity that is tenderness, I have thought,
Looking at these last stalls that I have wrought
This side of the chapter's octagon, I find
No hand but mine at work, yet mine refined
By yours, and all the difference: my motif
Of foliate form, your godliness in leaf.
        And your last spandrel proves the debt incurred
Not all on the one side. There I see a bird
Pecks at your grapes, and after him a fowler,
A boy with a bow. Elsewhere, your leaves discover
Of late blank mask-like faces. We infect
Each other then, doubtless to good effect . . .
And yet, take care: this cordial knack bereaves
The mind of all its sympathy with leaves,
Even with stone. I would not take away

From your peculiar mastery, if I say
A sort of coldness is the core of it,
A sort of cruelty; that prerequisite
Perhaps I rob you of, and in exchange give
What? Vulgarity's prerogative,
Indulgence towards the frailties it indulges,
Humour called 'wryness' that acknowledges
Its own complicity. I can keep in mind
So much at all events, can always find
Fallen humanity enough, in stone,
Yes, in the medium; where we cannot own
Crispness, compactness, elegance, but the feature
Seals it and signs it work of human nature
And fallen though redeemable. You, I fear,
Will find you bought humanity too dear
At the price of some light leaves, if you begin
To find your handling of them growing thin,
Insensitive, brittle. For the common touch,
Though it warms, coarsens. Never care so much
For leaves or people, but you care for stone
A little more. The medium is its own
Thing, and not all a medium, but the stuff
Of mountains; cruel, obdurate, and rough.

Under St Paul's

Wren and Barry, Rennie and Mylne and Dance
    Under the flags, the men who stood for stone
    Lie in the stone. Carillons, pigeons once
Sluiced Ludgate's issues daily, and the dome
    Of stone-revetted crystal swung and hung
    Its wealth of waters. Wren had plugged it home
With a crypt at the nerve of London. Now the gull
    Circles the dry stone nozzles of the belfries,
    Each graceful City hydrant of the full
Eagerly brimming measure of agreement,
    Still to be tapped by any well-disposed
    Conversible man, still underneath the pavement
Purling and running, affable and in earnest,
    The conduit, Candour. Fattily urbane
    Under the great drum, pigeons foul their nest.

The whiter wing, Anger, and the gull's
Shearwater raucous over hunting hulls
Seek London's river. Rivers underground,
Under the crypt, return the sound
Of footfalls in the evening city. Out of wells,
Churchyards sunk behind Fleet Street, trickle smells
Of water where a calm conviction spoke
Now dank and standing. Leaves and our debris choke
The bell-note Candour that the pavior heard
Fluting and swelling like a crop-filled bird.

So sound the tides of love; yet man and woman
    May be my world's first movers, and the stream
    Still run no darker nowhere deeper than
Conviction's claim upon us, to deny
    Nothing that's undeniable. Light airs
    Are bent to the birds that couple as they fly
And slide and soar, yet answer to the flow
    Of this broad water under. There we ride

Lent to the current, and convictions grow
In those they are meant for. As conviction's face
        Is darker than the speculative air,
        So and no darker is the place
For candour and love. What fowl lives underwater,
        Breeds in that dark? And hadn't a contriver
        Of alphabets, Cadmus, the gull for daughter?

Across the dark face of the waters
Flies the white bird. And the waters
Mount, mount, or should mount; we grow surer
Of what we know, if no surer
Of what we think. For on ageing
Labouring now and subsiding and nerveless wing
The gull sips the body of water, and the air
Packed at that level can hold up a minster in air.
Across the dark face of the water
Flies the white bird until nothing is left but the water.

St Paul's Revisited

'The change of Philomel, by the barbarous king,
So rudely forced'.
*[In the myth, Philomela became a nightingale, and
Tereus, her ravisher, a hoopoe.]*

Anger, a white wing? No, a hoopoe's wing,
King Tereus, Hatred. Crested ravisher,
The motley lapwing whoops and whoops it up
Greek Street and Fleet Street till the gutters run
Their serial feature. Liquid, yellow, thick,
It pools here, fed from the Antipodes,
The Antilles . . . For the seven seas run with bile
To the Pool of London, sink where the ordure, talent
At home in this world, gathers. And it pools
Not only there but in whatever head
Recalls with rage the choir of Christ and Wren.

Horned and self-soiling, not the barbarous king
Of Thrace and the anthologies, nor a brute,
A plain quick killer, but degenerate,
The rapist lapwings sideways through our heads
And finds no exit. There's a place it might:
The A-to-Z preserves no record of it
Though Strype or any antique gazetteer
Describes it well enough, a Thames-side borough
Decayed already, called Depravity.
If we could find it now, our hoopoes might
Hop from inside our heads, and Thames run cleaner.

Anger won't do it. Ire! Its hooked bill gouges
The chicken-livers of its young. Irate,
We are depraved, and by that token. Gulls
Cry, and they skeeter on a candid wing
Down slopes of air, but not for anger's sake.
Spite, malice, arrogance and 'Fuck you, Jack',
Birds in the gables of Depravity

Twitter and cheep, but most inside my head
And can be lived with. But the hoopoe whoops
Always inside, and rancorous. Rancour! Rancour!
Oh patriotic and indignant bird!

Vying

Vying is our trouble;
And a devious vice it is
When we vie in abnegations,
Services, sacrifices.

Not to be devious now
(For perhaps I should not begin
Taking the blame for winning
If this were not how to win),

I assert that such is the case:
I seem to have more resources;
I thrive on enforcing the more
The less naked the force is.

Mutinies, sulks, reprisals
All play into my hand;
To be injured and forgiving
Was one of the roles I planned.

Married to me, you take
The station I command,
As if in a peopled graveyard
Deserted in an upland.

There I, the sexton, battle
Earth that will overturn
Headstones, and rifle tombs,
And spill the tilted urn.

To Certain English Poets

My dears, don't I know? I esteem you more than you think,
    you modest and quietly spoken, you stubborn and unpersuaded.
    Your civil dislikes hum over a base that others
    shudder at, as at some infernal cold.
But pits full of smoky flame are sunk in the English Gehenna,
    where suffering souls like ours are bound and planted
    now in the one hot spot, now in another.
The operator is an imagination of Dante
    that plucks us out of the one and plugs us at once in another
    with an obedient pip-pip-pip at the switchboard.
Like you I look with astonished fear and revulsion
    at the gross and bearded, articulate and good-humoured
    Franco-American torso, pinned across
    the plane of human action, twitching and roaring.
Yet a restlessness less than divine comes over us, doesn't it,
      sometimes,
    to string our whole frames, ours also, in scintillant items,
    with an unabashed crackle of intercom and static?
Or will you, contained, still burn with that surly pluck?

Brantôme

J'ai eu pitié des autres.
Pas assez.
          (*The Pisan Cantos*)

Burly, provincial France,
Your rarefied, severe
Renaissance is
Material and four-square
Here, in a stout arrangement
Of water, stone and grass
Where the unlettered can
Come and read in the clear
Air of a weeping April
Thus rendered, the austere
Theorems of the jurist
Or fierce geometer.

I walk your foreign turf.
My native tongue was leased
Fawningly, long ago,
To the too long appeased
Long pitied vulgar. I
Speak to myself in French,
Thinking myself in a place
Where a lettered man's remorse
For intellectual pride
And ruthlessness of the mind
May be accepted, not
Pounced on and misapplied.

'Abbeyforde'

Thirty years unremembered,
Monkey-faced black-bead-silken
Great-aunt I sat across from,
Gaping and apprehensive,
The thought of you suddenly fits.
Across great distances
Clement time brings in its
Amnesties, Aunt Em.

'Abbeyforde': the name
Decyphered stood for Ford
Abbey, in Somerset. There
Your brother's sweetheart Nell,
My grandmother, drew him to her,
Whom later he pitchforked North.
Such dissolutions, Em!
Such fatal distances!

'Keep still feast for ever . . .'
A glow comes up off the page
In which I read of a paschal
Feast of the diaspora
In Italy, in a bad
Time for the Jews, and it is
As if in that tender and sad
Light your face were illumined.

Commodore Barry

When Owen Roe
O'Sullivan sang Ho
For the hearts of oak
Of broken Thomond, though
Weevils and buggery should
Have wormed the wooden walls
More than De Grasse's cannon,
The sweetest of the masters
Of Gaelic verse in his time,
Lame rhymester in English, served
And laurelled Rodney's gun.

Available as ever
Implausibly, the Stuart
Claimed from the Roman stews
His sovereignty *de jure*;
But Paddy, in the packed
Orlop, the *de facto*
Sovereignty of ordure,
King George's, had to hedge
His bet upon a press
Of white legitimist sail
Off Kinsale, some morning.

A flurry of whitecaps off
The capes of the Delaware!
Barry, the Irish stud,
Has fathered the entire
American navy! Tories
Ashore pore over the stud-book,
Looking in vain for the mare,
Sovran, whom Jolly Roger
Of Wexford or Kildare
Claims in unnatural congress
He has made big with frigates.

Loyalists rate John
Paul Jones and Barry, traitors;
One Scotch, one Irish, pirate.
In Catherine the Great's
Navy, her British captains
Years later refused to sail with
The Scot-free renegade. Jones
And Barry took the plunge
Right, when the sovereigns spun;
Plenty of Irish pluck
Called wrong, was not so lucky.

'*My* sovereign,' said saucy
Jack Barry, meaning Congress;
And yes, it's true, outside
The untried, unstable recess
Of the classroom, every one has one:
A sovereign – general issue,
Like the identity-disc,
The prophylactic, the iron
Rations. Irony fails us,
Butters no parsnips, brails
No sail on a ship of the line.

My Father's Honour

Dim in the glimmering room
Over against my bed . . .
Astonished awake, I held
My breath to see my dead,
My green-eyed, talkative
Dead father come.

That look he has! A rare one
In a vivacious man.
I grasp at the uncommon
Identifiable look,
Reproach. The charge it levels
Is no unfair one.

Hold to that guise, reproach,
Cat's eyes! Eerily glow,
Green, prominent, liquid;
Level the charge, although
I could not have done other,
And this you know.

Hold there, green eyes! But no,
Upon the nebulous ground
His merciful nature cuts
From shot to genial shot,
Indulgent now, as if
In honour bound.

Christmas Syllabics for a Wife

When I think of you
dying before or
after me, I am
ashamed how little
there is for either
one of us to look
back upon as done
wholly in concert.

We have spent our lives
arming for them. Now
we see they begin
to be over, and
now is it too late
to profit by what
seems to have been a
long preparation?

The certainty that
many have scaped scot-
free or even praised
sets the adrenalin
anger flushing up
through me as often
before, but can we
wait now for justice?

Horace says, Be wise
broach the ripe wine and
carefully decant
it. Now is the time
to measure wishes
by what life has to
give. Not much. So be
from now on greedy.

Emigrant, to the Receding Shore

for the shade of Herbert Read

The weather of living in an island
That is not an island in the ocean
Crackles in the hallway. What is salt
And ancient in us dries
To an inland heat. The Atlantic
Is a pond sunk in a garden,
A concrete mole has sealed the Aleutian vents
Browned already; only beside New Zealand
Perhaps do sobs refresh
A walled-up bind of waters.

Alfred in Athelney, Hereward in the Isle
Of Ely, learn to go mounted.

Tooling through second-growth Sherwood
In an Armstrong-Siddeley tourer,
Percheron of the 'twenties,
My grandfather unmeaning
Anything but well
Discharged his quiverful:
Aridity, and levels.

The anti-cyclone regions
Of population pressure,
Respondent to the pulse of
Asia, Arabia, Kansas,
Send out their motorized
Hordes, the freely breeding.

And the Age of Chivalry prinks
Pygmy-size to my daughter's
Gymkhana, though the Godolphin
Arabian has invaded

The forested, painfully cleared
Lands of the Clydesdale, the Suffolk
And the Shire horse, the old black English.
The great trees sail the oceans,
Spill acorns on Pitcairn Island.
And all of this is over.

Trevenen

I

His Return (Christmas, 1780)

Winds from Cook's Strait cannot blow
Hard enough to lift the snow
Already comfortably deep
Where Roseveare and Treyarnon sleep;
Knit to the centre from the far
Fastness of their peninsula,
The Cornish dream that distance can
Deliver their young gentleman
Unaltered to his mother's arms,
To be in rectories and farms,
Assembly-rooms and markets, shown
As the great Cook's and yet their own.
        Camborne's as certain as St James
That vocabulary tames
The most outlandish latitude;
That, at a pinch, to speak of rude
Hardihood will meet the case
And teach a Bligh to know his place;
And 'gallant' and 'ingenious' will
Confine their irrepressible
Midshipman who murders sleep,
Sprung from the London coach to heap
His hero-worship of the dead
Hero on each doting head.
        It would be years before he knew
Himself what it had brought him to;
What it had meant, his profiting
By the good offices of King
And Bligh, the mote-dance in the air
Of their vacated cabins where
Sea-glitters pulsed above his head
Bent to his books. And loving dread

Of his commander's furies taught
Lessons of another sort
If he could trust to having seen
How far from rational and serene
Command might be. When, at the oar
Under Cook's marginally more
Indulgent but still beetling eye,
He clawed a cutter round the high
Northwestern overhang, it meant
The profile of a continent.
So much he knew, and knew with pride;
And yet he was not satisfied,
Not now, nor later. But for now
He chatters to his mother how
Captain King he can instate
As the dead Cook's surrogate:
King, with his connections; King
In Ireland now and finishing
The narrative of the fatal cruise
(Awaited, though no longer news);
King, and his kindness (Bligh, the spurned,
Unconnected patron, burned
With a jealousy that seared
King's account, when it appeared,
With marginalia . . .); King, whose eyes
Smiled on skill and enterprise
Such as young Trevenen knew
He could boast, and ardour too;
Sweet James King, whom more than one
Hawaiian wanted for a son;
King, then (and so the plaudits end)
At once a mentor and a friend,
Rare composite of gall and balm,
Skilful to command and charm.
       Thus, mixed with talk of azimuth
And quadrant, to confound Redruth,
Trevenen, merrily enough,

Talks of how it merits love,
Some men's authority; and some
Clerical auditors keep mum,
Shocked to know how near they come
To greeting (so enthralled they are)
With an impious 'huzzah'
Such a sublime condition as
They've pressed on their parishioners
As more than human. 'Well, but no,'
They tell themselves, 'the boy don't know
How near he grazes Gospel-truth.
Brave spirit of ingenuous youth!'
And so they huff and puff it home
With (to their wives) 'Come, madam, come!'
Their wives and daughters half aware
Dear Papa has an absent air.

     It troubles him, as well it might,
To see in such resplendent light
Mortal redeemers crowd upon
A stage that should be cleared for One,
That One, Divine. There was some doubt
Whether Cook had been devout;
Though as to that one could not feel
Happy with excess of zeal,
Remembering saintly Wesley whose
Vexatiousness had emptied pews
Down all the stolid Duchy, packed
Gwennap Pit, and loosed in fact
Who knew what furies in deluded
Tin-mine Messiahs? So he brooded,
The honest rector. As for that,
He thought, there's worse to wonder at:
Wrong principles inflame and spread
When they aureole a head
Rank has exalted more than those
Who merely by their talents rose.
Thus, nothing's more alarming than

That too warm Christian gentleman,
Lord George Gordon, the inspired
And loved authority that fired
Prison and church, and did not spare
Lord Mansfield's house in Bloomsbury Square . . .
'Bah!' he thought, 'what has all this
To do with young men's loyalties?'

II

Life and Contacts (1784–7)

The poet Crabbe, with whom he shared
Burke as patron, never cared
(It appears) to throw a frame
Round the poems that made his fame.
There, as if through window-glass,
Men like James Trevenen pass
Plain and unflattered. Never mind
Asking what poetic kind
Crabbe's tales belong to; they escape
Any predetermined shape,
Comic, heroic, or whatever.
Pointing morals was, however,
Crabbe's substitute. Subtitled 'Or
Hero-worship', would a more
Rationally pleasing piece,
With less of oddity and caprice
In the conduct of it, come
Of this that we're embarked upon?
Hardly: morals underlined
Outrage our taste. Besides, my mind
Is far from made up in this case
About what moral we should trace
In a story that is more
Painful than I've prepared you for.
– First, the untimely death of King.

His malady was lingering,
And yet did not take very long
Once it attacked the second lung.
Then, the death of brother Matt
At twenty-three, beleaguered at
Okehampton in the inn, who trolled,
'Unlike the ladies of the old
Times', his song; 'their hue unfaded
That needed no calash to shade it . . .'
The light young tenor 'of the old
Times, the old ancient ladies' told,
Echoing in a brother's head
Cracked gaiety, the singer dead.
    A man, thus severally bereaved,
Labours not to be deceived
By smiling seas of Life, nor Art's
Flattering pledge to furnish charts.
And no such suave commitment mars
Crabbe, the realist *sans phrase* . . .
Perhaps had Johnson lived, whose pen
Tinkered with *The Village*, then
Some one had upheld the claims
Of spectacles defined by frames,
Or songs like Matthew's, set to airs
Traditional at country fairs;
But Johnson died, unwept by most,
And left, to rule the sprawling roost,
Crabbe's earnest, just, unfocussed page
As prolix model to an age
Which, fed on ornament, would brook
Pindaric Odes to Captain Cook
And, stretched on Ossian, did not shirk
Orations paced by Fox and Burke:
Splendid, sublime and fervent, strong
In argument, but long, but long.
    Apart from that, it can be shown
To have been an age much like our own;

As lax, as vulgar, as confused;
Its freedoms just as much abused;
Where tattle stole a hero's thunder,
His death a thrill, and nine days' wonder;
Where personalities were made,
And makers of them plied a trade
Profitable and esteemed;
Where that which was and that which seemed
Were priced the same; where men were duped
And knew they were, and felt recouped
By being town-talk for a day,
Their Gothic follies on display;
Where (and here the parallel
Comes home, I hope, and hurts as well)
Few things met with such success
As indignant righteousness.
        Burke's the paradigm of this,
Hissing at enormities
In India, at Westminster-hall
(Holy debauch, a free-for-all);
A man of principle, not able
(Like Fox, who had the gaming-table
To share his heart with politics)
To guard against the squalid tricks
That Tender Conscience and Just Rage
Play, when on a public stage;
Not keeping, in his fevered heart,
Passion and Principle apart;
But purchasing his never too
Much honoured sense of what was due
To private merit and indeed
Domestic virtue, by a need
To compensate for his serene
Privacies by public spleen . . .
        To King, the friend of Irish friends,
Burke gives a bed, and Jane Burke tends
His hopeless case. And King's release

Comes in that same year, in Nice,
Whither Trevenen had, with one
Other, conveyed him, to the sun.
        The Burkes had sent him; and he rode
Back to them, slowly, overshadowed
Thenceforward, always, by a sense
Of human life's inconsequence.
        No man more worthy of his trust,
It might be thought – nor, if he must
Still worship, of his worship – than
The great, good Anglo-Irishman,
Edmund Burke. Secure within
That circle, guest of Inchiquin
At Cliefden, or else entertained
At Gregories itself, he gained
Dubious information how
Iniquitous were Pitt and Howe;
How unregarded was the merit
Of Cook, of King; how to inherit
Their mantle meant he must not hope
For advancement of much scope.
At other times the conversation
Was a liberal education
In men and manners; how Lord George
Gordon, once again at large
(Though, some years before, expelled
From this circle) was impelled
By honour when for the disbanded
Mariners he had demanded,
The year before, some action such
As could have shipped them for the Dutch;
How Cowper, in *The Task*, confessed
To remaining unimpressed
By the reasons given for
Incursions on Tahiti's shore;
How fractious Barry must be borne with,
Painting lineaments of myth

For all his tantrums, the antique
Burning his style down to the Greek;
How Nollekens had little sense
Of decency, yet could dispense
With it, to mould a *busto*; how
Cagliostro made his bow;
How civil good Sir Joshua was,
And Admiral Saunders; how, across
A field from where they sat, was found
The plot of venerable ground
Where slippery Waller lay; and how
Illiberal was Pitt, was Howe . . .
    Small wonder if his head was turned,
If a renewed resentment burned
In him to sell his rusting sword
Wherever sovereigns could afford
Ensigns announcing to the gale
Citizens of the world in sail.
Bligh gets the *Bounty*, and not he;
He's pledged himself to Muscovy.

III

His End (The Battle of Viborg, 21 June 1790)

Long, splendid shadows! Cornwall, lit
Bronze in the evening, levels it
Off, and pays all; the yea or nay
Of switched allegiance, as the day
Dies on the old church-tower, seems
A dilemma of our dreams
Which, however urgent once,
Awake we need not countenance.
The gilding beams that reconcile
This antique issue, can for mile
On cloud-racked mile slant on, to reach
Amber on a Baltic beach . . .

Apollonian, reconciling
Art, that is drenched in tears, yet smiling!
Persuading us to think all's one,
Lit by a declining sun.
      Not for George Crabbe! His it is
To give untinged veracities;
And, though it's Christian, this indeed
Our baffled heroes seem to need,
Moving to their wasteful ends,
Betrayed by principles and friends –

        Cold and pain in the breast,
        Fatigue drives him to rest.
        Rising, 'to open a new
        Source of comfort to you'
        (Writing to his wife
        The last night of his life),
        Captain Trevenen, sick,
        Wears on no other tack,
        Aware man's born to err,
        Inclined to bear and forbear.
        Pretence to more is vain.
        Chastened have they been.
        Hope was the tempter, hope.
        Ambition has its scope
        (Vast: the world's esteem);
        Hope is a sickly dream.
        And seeking, while they live,
        Happiness positive
        Is sinful. Virtue alone –
        This they have always known –
        Is happiness below.
        Therefore, she is to know,
        Whatever is, is right.
        That solid, serious light
        Shall reconcile her to
        Candidacy below

For where his sails are furled,
Far from fame and the world.

Camborne's rector would have seen
Comfort in the ghastly scene,
There in the British burial-ground
In summery Kronstadt, had he found
His son so firm, and yet so meek.
So truly Christian, truly bleak
The sentiments a man should speak,
Meeting his Maker! In our eyes
A man we cannot recognize
As Burke's or King's accomplished friend,
Cowed mumbler from the sealed-off end
Of Celtic England, glares and points;
And this raw difference disjoints
Our and Elegy's specious frame,
Framing all our deaths the same
(Our loves, our worships, levelled in
The eyes of Art, that Jacobin).
        Lord George Gordon! he was found
Worshipful, the country round,
Some years before. Now no one hears
His civilly enounced ideas
Without reserve. But when, as host,
He gives his Radicals their toast,
'Mr Burke! who has afforded
Grounds for discussion', he's applauded.
And, sure enough, we well may find
Burke and the Jacobins of one mind,
One self-same ruinous frame, unless
We recollect that Burke could bless
Those death-bed words from one whose head
He may have turned, whom he misled:
        'Though Will finds worldly scope,
        We have no earthly hope.'
Edmund Burke had cried, 'Amen!'
And James King, and most other men.

The Year 1812

Year well remembered! Happy who beheld thee!
The commons knew thee as the year of yield,
But as the year of war, the soldiery.

Rumours and skyward prodigies revealed
The poet's dream, the tale on old men's lips,
The spring when kine preferred the barren field.

Short of the acres green with growing tips
They halted lowing, chewed the winter's cud;
The men awaited an apocalypse.

Languid the farmer sought his livelihood
And checked his team and gazed, as if enquiring
What marvels gathered westward while he stood.

He asked the stork, whose white returning wing
Already spread above its native pine
Had raised the early standard of the Spring.

From swallows gathering frozen mud to line
Their tiny homes, or in loud regiments
Ranged over water, he implored a sign.

The thickets hear each night as dusk descends
The woodcock's call. The forests hear the geese
Honk, and go down. The crane's voice never ends.

What storms have whirled them from what shaken seas,
The watchers ask, that they should come so soon?
Or in the feathered world, what mutinies?

For now fresh migrants of a brighter plume
Than finch or plover gleam above the hills,
Impend, descend, and on our meadows loom.

Cavalry! Troop after troop it spills
With strange insignia, strangely armed,
As snow in a spring thaw fills

The valley roads. From the forests long
Bright bayonets issue, as brigades of foot
Debouch like ants, form up, and densely throng;

All heading north as if the bird, the scout,
Had led men here from halcyon lands, impelled
By instincts too imperative to doubt.

War! the war! – a meaning that transpires
To the remotest corner. In the wood
Beyond whose bounds no rustic mind enquires,

Where in the sky the peasant understood
Only the wind's cry, and on earth the brute's
(And all his visitors the neighbourhood),

A sudden glare! A crash! A ball that shoots
Far from the field, makes its impeded way,
Rips through the branches and lays bare the roots.

The bearded bison trembles, and at bay
Heaves to his forelegs, ruffs his mane, and glares
At sudden sparks that glitter on the spray.

The stray bomb spins and hisses; as he stares,
Bursts. And the beast that never knew alarm
Blunders in panic to profounder lairs.

'Whither the battle?' – and the young men arm.
The women pray, 'God is Napoleon's shield,
Napoleon ours', as to the outcome calm.

Spring well remembered! Happy who saw thee then,
Spring of the war, Spring of the mighty yield,
That promised corn but ripened into men.

                    *   *   *

Out of the moist dark
Dawn without glow brings
Day without brightness.

Sunrise, a whiteness
In a thatch of mist,
Shows late to eastward.

Earth is as tardy;
Cows go to pasture,
Startle hares grazing.

Fog that had spared them
Dayspring's alarum
Dispels them with herds.

Groves where the damp birds
Brood are their havens
In the still woodland.

Storks clack from marshland;
Ravens on haycocks
Croak of wet weather.

Scythes ring together,
Clink of the sickle,
Hone, hammer, and dirge.

Fog at the field's verge
Strangles the echo
Of labour and song.

The bravery of its gentry,
The beauty of their women
Exalt Dobrzyn
Through Lithuania. Once
Six hundred gentry armed
Answered the summons,
The besom made of twigs;
But now no easy living
For gentry of Dobrzyn

In magnates' households,
In troops or at assemblies –
Like serfs they work their way,
Not clad like serfs, the men
In gowns black-striped on white,
In gloves their women spinning
Or leather-shod tending the herds.

All Bartlemies, Matthiases,
Of Polish stock,
Masovian still
In speech and usages,
Black-haired and aquiline,
Nicknamed to save confusion;
Their patriarch, Matthias,
'The Maciek of Macieks';
His house, although untended,
Their Capitol.

Mercury's vivid fringe,
Mullein and crocus bow
The thatch; and mosses tinge
The roof as green as tin.
The rabbit mines below
Windows where birds fly in.
Birdcage or warren now
The fortress of Dobrzyn.

Where once the gate would creak,
Swedes left a cannon ball.
Unhallowed crosses speak
Of sudden obsequies.
Specks swarm on every wall
And seem a rash of fleas;
In each there nests a ball
As in earth burrows, bees.

Innocent every door
Of nail or hook or latch.
(The steel old swordsmen wore
Bit iron, and stood the test
Nor ever showed a notch.)
Above, Dobrzynski crests;
Cheeses the bearings smutch
And swallows blur with nests.

Four helms, once ornaments
Of martial brows, the dove,
Love's votary, frequents;
A corselet of chain mail
Hangs as a chute above
A horse's stall; a tail
Lopped from the charger of
The Ottoman cleans a pail.

Ceres has banished Mars;
Vertumnus and Pomona
And Flora heal the scars
On stable, house and barn.
Today shall they throw over
That distaff rule, and learn
Old habits to recover
To greet the god's return.

*   *   *

Fair weather, and the day breaking
Day of our Lady of Flowers;
The sky clear, hung over land
Like a sea curved forward and backward;
Pearls under its wave
Some few stars still, though paling;
White cloudlet alone
(Wing feathers fray out in the azure),
Spirit departing
Belated by prayers,
Fares fast to its heavenly fellows.

Pearls dim and go out in the deep.
Pallor on the sky's brow midmost
Spreads, and one temple is swarthy
Crumpled, pillowed on shadows,
The other ruddy. The distant
Horizon parts like a lid
On the white of an eye
Iris and pupil, and a ray circles
Dazzles, a gold shaft
Stuck through the heart of a cloud.

Fires cluster and dart
Cross over, light over light
Overarches the sky-round;
Drowsy, a broken
Light under lashes shaken
The eye of the sun rose up
Glittered, seven-tinted:
Sapphire by blood is to ruby
Ruby by yellow to topaz
Crystal, by lucent
To diamond, and by flame
Great moon or fitful star.
And the eye of the sun rose up
Alone across the unmeasured.

Northamptonshire

King's Cliffe, in the evening: that Northampton stone
As fine as Cotswold, and more masculine . . .

Turpin on wheels, my long-lost self that rode
Southward the Great North Road, and had

This bourne in mind, that night was disconcerted:
Youth hostel, yes; also a sort of shrine.

To William Law! Well, later on I learned
To gut that author for my purposes.

Questions remain, however. William Law,
Saint of the English Church . . . And what is sainthood?

Some leading questions must be answered soon,
Lead where they will, scared schoolboy, where they will!

Oxfordshire

'Start such a fire in England, Master Ridley,
As shall not be put out' – the coupled martyrs
That Oxford steers by in its Morris Minors
Fried for a quibble in Scripture or Canon Law!

Saints we remember, must we remember martyrs?
Baptists though we were, I knew from childhood
Latimer's words, and knew the fire he meant:
Godly work, the pious Reformation.

Crucifixions! Hideousness of burning,
Sizzle of fats, the hideous martyrdoms:
Palach consumed in Prague, a human torch;
A Saigon Buddhist, robe a more lambent saffron;

Dead for a country, dead for a Constitution
(Allende, in his mouth the emptied chamber
Of prompt and fluent deputies), were these
Crucifixions? They were suicides.

'Martyrs may seek their death, but may not seize it . . .'
Fine scruples, fine distinctions! Can there be
Any too fine for fine-toned Oxford, in
The smell of roast meat and the glare of torches?

Suffolk

Something gone, something gone out with Nelson,
With him or by him. Something in its place:
A Dynamo! Broke of the Shannon takes,
Crippled in his retirement, a sedate
Pride in totting up the butcher's bills
Of single-ship engagements, finds his own
(His head still singing from an American cutlass)
The bloodiest yet. Audacity of Nelson
Sired Broke and calloused him; Jane Austen's hero,
Honourable, monogamous and sober,
Gunnery-expert, servant of the State,
His small estate was somewhere here, in Suffolk.
A better image should be found for it.

My education gave me this bad habit
Of reading history for a hidden plot
And finding it; invariably the same one,
Its fraudulent title always, 'Something Gone'.

Gainsborough might have painted him, with his
Wife and children and a sleek retriever
(Thomas Gainsborough, born at Sudbury)
In a less glaring light, a truer one.

The Harrow

Unimaginable beings –
Our own dead friends, the dead
Notabilities, mourned and mourning,
Hallam and Tennyson . . . is it
Our loss of them that harrows?

Or is it not rather
Our loss of images for them?
The continued being of Claude
Simpson can be imagined.
We cannot imagine its mode.

Us too in this He harrows. It is not
Only on Easter Saturday
That it is harrowing
To think of Mother dead,
To think, and not to imagine.

He descended into –
Not into Hell but
Into the field of the dead
Where he roughs them up like a tractor
Dragging its tray of links.

Up and down the field, a tender bruising,
A rolling rug of iron, for the dead
Them also, the Virtuous Pagans
And others, He came, He comes
On Easter Saturday and

Not only then He comes
Harrowing them – that they,
In case they doubted it, may
Quicken and in more
Than our stale memories stir.

The Departed

They see his face!

Live in the light of . . .

Such shadows as they must
cast, sharp-edged;
the whole floor, said to be crystal,
barry with them. And long!

Spokes that reach even to us,
pinned as we are to the rim.

His Themes

(after reading Edmond Jabès)

His themes? Ah yes he had themes.
It was what we all liked about him.
Especially I liked it.
One knew, nearly always one knew
what he was talking about, and he talked
in such a ringing voice.

What did he talk about? What,
just what were his themes?
Oh, of the most important!

Loss was one of his themes;
he told us, as any bard should,
      the story of our people
      (tribe), he had memorised
      chronologies, genealogies,
      the names and deeds of heroes,
      the succession of our kings,
      our priests, the sept of our pipers,
      the mediations . . . and this
      while, young and old,
      we extolled the immediate, meaning
      the unremembering. *Yes,*
      and what was his theme? His theme, you said, was . . .?

Loss. Loss was his theme.

And duty. He taught us our duty;
he taught us, as any
legislator should,
      the rules of hygiene, the clean
      and the unclean meats, the times and
      the means of fumigation,
      the strewing and spreading, of fires,

and what to do with the old
and how to dispose of the dead
and how to live with our losses
uncomplaining . . . and this
while, young and old,
we did our best to be free,
meaning unruly. *Yes,*
and what was his theme? What did you say his theme was?

Duty. His theme was duty.

Fear also. Fear was a theme;
he taught us, as all seers must,
continual apprehension:
> of one another, of
> our womenfolk and our
> male children, of
> the next clan over the mountains
> and of the mountains, also
> the waters, the heavenly bodies
> wheeling and colliding,
> of the wild beasts both large
> and infinitesimal, of
> revenants and of the future,
> and of the structure of matter
> and of the unknown . . . and all this
> while, young and old,
> we tried to keep our nerve,
> meaning, to be heedless. *Yes,*
> *and what was the theme, did you say, of this voice both*
> *hollow and ringing?*

Fear. Fear was the theme.

We like to be told these things.
We need to be reminded.

He sounds like a sort of priest.
What was your priesthood doing?

Nonsensical things, like spinning
a shallow great bowl of words
poised on the stick of a question,
pointing it this way and that
for an answering flash, as the bend
of a river may come in a flash
over miles and miles
from a fold in the hills, over miles.

We paid them no attention.

Advent

Some I perceive, content
And stable in themselves
And in their place, on whom
One that I know casts doubt;
Knowing himself of those
No sooner settled in
Than itching to get out.

I hear and partly know
Of others, fearless and
Flinging out, whom one
I know tries to despise;
Knowing himself of those
No sooner loosed than they
Weeping sue for the leash.

Some I see live snug,
Embosomed. One I know
Maunders, is mutinous,
Is never loved enough;
Being of those who are
No sooner safely lodged
They chafe at cherishing.

Some I know who seem
Always in keeping, whom
One I know better blusters
He will not emulate;
Being of those who keep
At Advent, Whitsuntide,
And Harvest Home in Lent.

Some who are his kin
Have strewn the expectant floor
With rushes, long before
The striding shadow grows
And grows above them; he,
The deeper the hush settles,
Bustles about more business.

The eclipse draws near as he
Scuttles from patch to shrinking
Patch of the wintry light,
Chattering, gnashing, not
Oh not to be forced to his knees
By One who, turned to, brings
All quietness and ease.

Self-contradictions, I
Have heard, do not bewilder
That providential care.
Switch and reverse as he
Will, this one I know,
One whose need meets his
Prevents him everywhere.

Devil on Ice

Called out on Christmas Eve for a working-party,
Barging and cursing, carting the wardroom's gin
To save us all from sin and shame, through snow,
The night unclear, the temperature sub-zero,
           Oh I was a bombardier
           For any one's Angry Brigade
That Christmas more than thirty years ago!

Later, among us bawling beasts was born
The holy babe, and lordling Lucifer
With him alas, that blessed morn. And so
Easy it was, I recognise and know
           Myself the mutineer
           Whose own stale bawdry helped
Salute the happy morn, those years ago.

Red Army Faction could have had me then;
Not an intrepid operative, but glib,
A character-assassin primed to go,
Ripe for the irreplaceable though low
           Office of pamphleteer.
           Father of lies, I knew
My plausible sire, those Christmases ago.

For years now I have been amenable,
Equable, a friend of law and order,
Devil on ice. Comes Christmas Eve . . . and lo!
A babe we laud in baby-talk. His foe
           And ours, not quite his peer
           But his antagonist,
Hisses and walks on ice, as long ago.

A Liverpool Epistle

to J.A. Steers, Esq, author of
The Coastline of England and Wales

Alfred, this couple here –
My son, your daughter – are
Can we deny it? strangers
To both of us. Ageing, I
Find I take many a leaf
Out of the useful book
Of your behaviour. 'Prof.',
Your title for years, becomes
Me, or meets my need;
Mask for what heartaches, what
Uncertain, instantaneous
(Panicky sometimes)
Judgments how to behave in
This net we seem to have woven
Between us, or been caught in.

Under a rusty gown not
Actual but conjured
By our behaviour, what
In some diminished sense
Compromising situations we
Either escape, or handle! Still,
Today I was found at a loss,
Confronted with the local
University's stalwarts
Of a past age: Bernard Pares,
Oliver Elton, George
Sampson, Fitzmaurice-Kelly . . .
Not that they did not deserve
Attention, there in their daubed
Likenesses; but how?
What was required of 'the Prof'?

In the event I managed
Well enough by my
Lenient expectations, but
I had such a sense of how
Tragical, one might say,
Our occupation is
Or may be. How
Beset it is, after all,
How very far from 'secluded',
This life of the scholar my son
And your daughter have followed us into!

It was explained to me,
For instance, there was one
Liverpool professor
Had had to be painted out
Of the group-portrait: Kuno
Meyer, Professor of German,
Whose notable devotion
To Ancient Irish took,
Come 1914, rather
A different colour. He
Declared himself for his Kaiser
Belligerently. And I
Must admit I am baffled:
Passion also has its
Claims upon us, surely;
Even the sort that is called,
Smirkingly, 'patriotic'.

Kenneth Allott, a poet
I think you will not have read,
Gave us ('I give you,' he wrote)
'The riotous gulls and the men
Crumpled, hat-clutching, in the wind's
Rages, and the shifting river',
Giving us Liverpool. Here

Anyone must be prompted
To solemn reflections in
A wind that must seem like the wind
Of history, blowing the chemical
Reek out of Runcorn over
The eerily unfrequented,
Once so populous, Mersey.

Cold hearth of empire, whose
Rasping cinders bring
Our erudite concerns
Home to us, with such
Asperity! This is
Liverpool, one enormous
Image of dereliction
Where yet our children warm themselves
And so warm us. We too
Are netted into it – you
Known as the protector
Of England's coastline, and
I, supposedly
Custodian of that other
Line around England: verse.

This turns, of course. Yes, one
Verse-line turns into the next
As Rodney Street into a slum, or
Philologists into Prussians;
Turnings in time as your
Headlands and bays are turnings
In space. A bittersweet pleasure
At best one takes in these
Revolutions, reversals,
Verses, whereas
The veerings of a coastline
(Seen from a lowflying aircraft,
A coastal road or, best,

A coasting ship) must be
Experienced, I think, as
A solemn sweetness always.

As prose at its saddest is less
Sorrowful than verse is
Necessarily, so
Geography, I have long
Thought, must be a sweeter
Study than history; sweeter
Because less cordial, less
Of heartbreak in it. More
Human warmth, it follows,
Is possible or common
In Liverpool than in
Some spick-and-span, intact,
Still affluent city. So
The warmth of our children's household
For the time being persuades me.

Fare Thee Well

Bideford! Nothing will do
To make the place ring true
To its after-rain luminous presence
That day last summer, so
Precipitous, tempest-whipped
As that summer was to us two,
And as Bideford was also
That day we were there,

But embarkations: faces
Cheese-white in lamplight; lights
Dancing on blackness as
They rock away; oars are shipped,
'Ahoy!' and an answering growl,
And they climb aboard, and the wicker
Basket and bird-cage are
Hoist in; and the anchor is tripped.

Make what you will of the figure
Of outward, I cannot afford
To let you go, to unloose you
To that all-levelling
Hardship of ocean. See!
Some one has cast a hawser,
Some one has caught it. Wrapped
On a bollard, it checks, it is gripped.

Oh it is you I would check.
When it comes to the outward bound,
You are to be outstripped:
Farewell! I am far down the Sound,
Dwindled, my moorings slipped.
Somewhere by Barnstaple Bay
I have embraced you, I turn
Seaward. 'Farewell,' I say.

Because in the event
The hawser will not be bent
Nor gripped so handily, and
Goodbyes will be untoward
In some more sterilised place
Than Bideford, accept
This easy rehearsal: that when
The time comes, we be equipped.

Some Future Moon

after Pasternak

Before me a far-off time arises
Far in the future. You,
Whoever you are, are mine;
This is to say I know you.

The sodium street-lights beam
On to a stonescape as
Remote from the Plymouth I know
As mine from Frobisher's.

You are a girl or a boy;
All the same, one of the few.
Whoever you are, you are mine;
This is to say I claim you.

This which I need to tell you
Quietly is none
Other than what the Tamar
Shines to the Eddystone.

Listen! For the lisp of
The waters at Admiral's Hard
Decayed in my day already
Now can scarcely be heard.

They neither shine nor sound
Unless in a little tune
I name both them and you
And set you under the moon.

Watch with me how the moon
Sinks on Mount Edgecumbe. Think
How many lovers' joys
With that moon rose, and sink.

And yet think also how,
Whatever your war-machines
And your machine-made songs,
These are unchanging scenes:

Because I say so, Mount
Edgecumbe's shelving ground
Crowds to the dropping down
Of warships outward bound;

Because I say so, you
Unknown sit with me here,
Your eyes a-shine because
I will it so, my dear.

You have this world no man
Nor man's machine can take
Away from you because
I made it for your sake.

A Late Anniversary

Constant the waterman
Skims the red water
Of sunset river,
Singing to Marian
The miller's daughter.

Wharf nor weir on this
Stretch of the river, it pours
Mournful and nebulous, Time's
Unseizable accomplice.

Sing to her, waterman.
Woo her unfaltering,
Constant as best you can,
Self-same by altering.

Your traffic is yourself:
The sidelong pour off a shelf
Or the popple about a stone.
It is what she would wish,
You have to think.

Rousseau in His Day

So many nights the solitary lamp had burned;
So many nights his lone mind, slowing down
Deliberately, had questioned, as it turned
Mooning upon its drying stem, what arc
Over a lifetime day had moved him through.

Always he hoped he might deserve a Plutarch,
Not to be one posterity forgot.
Nor have we. He has left his mark: one tight
Inched-around circuit of the screw of light,
As glowing shadows track the life of roses
Over unchosen soil-crumbs. It was not
What he'd expected or the world supposes.

Portland

after Pasternak

Portland, the Isle of Portland – how I love
Not the place, its name! It is as if
These names were your name, and the cliff, the breaking
Of waves along a reach of tumbled stone
Were a configuration of your own
Firm slopes and curves – your clavicles, your shoulder.
A glimpse of that can set the hallway shaking.

And I am a night sky that is tired of shining,
Tired of its own hard brilliance, and I sink.

Tomorrow morning, grateful, I shall seem
Keen, but be less clear-headed than I think;
A brightness more than clarity will sail
Off lips that vapour formulations, make
Clear sound, full rhyme, and rational order take
Account of a dream, a sighing cry, a moan.

Like foam on all three sides at midnight lighting
Up, far off, a seaward jut of stone.

Grudging Respect

As when a ruined face
Lifted among those crowding
For the young squire's largesse
Perceives him recognise
Her and she grabs, not for any
Languidly lofted penny
They scrabble for, but for his eyes
And pockets them, their clouding
That instant; and the abruptness
With which his obliging is checked,
His suddenly leaving the place . . .

Just so may a grudging respect
Be, from a despised one,
Not just better than none
At all, but sweeter than any.

No Epitaph

No moss nor mottle stains
My parents' unmarked grave;
My word on them remains
Stouter than stone, you told me.

'Martyred to words', you have thought,
Should be your epitaph;
At other times you fought
My self-reproaches down.

Though bitterly once or twice
You have reproached me with how
Everything ended in words,
We both know better now:

You understand, I shall not
If I survive you care
To raise a headstone for
You I have carved on air.

Artifex in Extremis

In memoriam Howard Warshaw

Let him rehearse the gifts reserved for age
   Much as the poet Eliot did, but more
   Than thirty-five years after: . . . Rending rage
Discountenanced by his Church, the rent and sore
   Patient nods under gin or seconal
   Or his small fame, such drugs. His visitor,
The one and only in this hospital,
   Is nurse and woman. Time and time again
   She brings her numbing serum, whom to call
A button's by his bed. He calls her when,
   Ashamed, he feels his practised self-control
   Slipping a notch. Hotly he asks her then:
'Is there no choice? Am I to sell my soul
   Short, or fake it, for my nearest kin
   Forever, till I die?' Prompt on the whole
She brings her priceless needleful of guilt,
   Oblivion, and equality; his rôle
   Is possum, playing possum to the hilt.

The hilt, though, is a long way down and in;
   The whole blade is before it, going deep
   Bleeding and shearing. Though the mottled skin
Knits up and shines, the legless cries in his sleep
   For pain in the limb aborted. There was once,
   Torturing to remember, in that steep
Slope off to nowhere, stamping-ground and stance,
   Foothold, some hard earth under. He discerns
   Still many a cherished, hard-earned eminence
Loom from his past, on all of which by turns
   He took his stand. No need to specify.
   There is not one of them that now he spurns;
On all that ring of hills his drowsing eye
   Sees his young self still model rectitude
   Erect and certain. Clear against the sky

Above his drug-dimmed but still savage mood,
   Seen but by him, the things that he has held by
   Unchangeably enforce his solitude.

His arrogance is terrible to no one
   More than to him. It is incurable.
   The enormity of it ramrods bone on bone
When he stands up for anything at all,
   Rending both it and him. No palliation
   In trusting to posterity, at call
No longer for belated vindication;
   The future, if it comes (as he is not
   Sure that it will), will in his estimation
Be more obtuse, not less. His work is what
   Stands, but as if on Easter Island, rude
   And enigmatic effigies, a lot
Unsold at history's auction. When of crude
   Unlettered clergy Thomas Cranmer's prose
   Demands too much, what but desuetude
Attends one's best? This being what he knows,
   His own sick say-so and presumption can
   Alone sustain the artificer in the man.

Then why, he asks himself (his self-contempt
   Half self-pity), of late these reams on reams
   Addressed to a young kinsman? To attempt,
Having no heirs, to write one's will – it seems
   The enforced sell-out: exegetes pre-empt
   Prophecies, polemics serve for dreams,
And pedagogue supplants protagonist,
   As rhetoric, action. Always in the event
   One must, despite the lacerating twist
Of disbelief, limp to a testament
   Too shrill for dignity. Of late he's missed
   That most – the dignity. A low sun lent
Once or twice, his monumental forms
   Upon the hill-tops just the effect he meant:

Scrutable, yet unfathomable. Norms
Of expectation (anxious, confident,
    His kinsman's face . . .) obscure them; one performs
    Simply such things, intent, without intent.

For the most part now he drifts, his conduct as
    Considerate as has come to be expected,
    Querulous seldom. His *superbia* has
Been at such pains to ravage undetected
    (And swelled the more) that now he practises
    Unthinkingly the long ago perfected
Deceit of warming to the common touch,
    Much-loved, attentive. That too he has made
    A point of, staunchly – not to ask, for such
As he is, special licences. Betrayed
    By that pretence of unpretension, much
    As now he may regret the terms of trade
He fixed himself, he has to acquiesce
    When he perceives his own dear things are weighed
    And shelved at market-prices. To confess
The work that would, he thought, speak for itself
    Has not, comes hard. Benumbed, he stands himself,
    With all his other pieces, on the shelf.

'A good life,' he will tell me, 'though I wish . . .'
    And so on – much what anyone might say.
    Blind to his own case? Or this queerer fish
That terrifies me, reading him today
    Into myself tomorrow – which one thumbs
    The bedside button, and no woman comes?

Catullus on Friendship

'Cancel, Catullus, the expectancies of friendship
Cancel the kindnesses deemed to accrue there . . .'
                                        (tr. Peter Whigham)

It must make a great difference, having friends.
    Yeats had Pound and Pound had Yeats, and Frost
Had, briefly, Edward Thomas. It must make
    A world of difference, having trusted friends
And trustworthy – eh, my Lampadius?

It must make all the difference, having friends
    To be dealt with cleanly, honestly – must it not,
Busy Lampadius? Friends who are not too busy
    To recognise the claims one has on them,
The vise one has them in – that too of course.

A world, a world of difference, my
    Never quite trusted and yet far too trusted
Friend, Lampadius . . . One must rub along.
    Just so, just so; the debts of friendship must,
Given the state of the market, be adjusted.

Lampadius, you're a poet; a busy one,
    And not half bad. Whichever god you sing
Or speak to, it's a lonely business; if
    To no god but a friend, it's lonelier;
But loneliest when there's no one there but 'readers'.

What puzzles or intrigues me, then, is how
    Your busy-ness refuels. In our youth
Mere self-advancement is a sufficient target:
    The sort of fame that's 'being talked about'.
What kept you going when you'd tired of that?

A secret, and you'll keep it. I don't know
   Whether or not to envy you the possession
Of such pure fuel as it seems I never
   Had, or have lost. My name for it was 'friendship';
Which can't be right, I think when I think of you.

'Kindred souls' – a prettily old-fashioned
   Extravagant name for what we had and have,
A competition between siblings. Such
   Olympian squabbles as that phrase clears up,
Which exercised the ancestors so direly!

Cleared up, acknowledged, cleared away . . . And yet
   The gods help friendship, since the life-force holds
No stake in it. Lampadius, what I
   Mean to say is I can't sing or speak
When friends and kindred can be sold downriver.

Utterings

(Bird)   To flex in the upper airs
                    To the unseen but known
                    Velocity of change
                    That both prevails and gives –
                    If anything that lives
                    That is able to know it, knows
                    Better to bend to the press
                    Of need, and so command it,
                    Him I envy, his
                    So much more strait duress.

(Salmon)   Pressures, pressures of water,
                    Of running water, because
                    As needs must downward driving,
                    Define imperatives.
                    If anything that lives
                    That is able to know it, knows
                    Better than I do the spine
                    Set taut against the grab
                    Of gravity, that thing knows
                    More happiness than mine.

(Man)   Making your own mistakes
                    And living the blame of them, making
                    The same ones time after time,
                    Which nobody forgives –
                    If anything that lives
                    That is able to know it, knows
                    A better happiness than
                    This – and he is Legion
                    That thinks he does – he is
                    Disranked from the branch of Man.

(Angel)   On us no pressures, none.
                 Adoration is
                 Not required, but what
                 Each one desirously gives.
                 If anything that lives
                 That is able to know it, knows
                 A better happiness, then
                 The frame of the world is askew;
                 I share the happiness
                 Of salmon, birds, and men.

(Sheepdog/   Knowing your own business,
Artist)   And such a delicate business;
                 Uttering it with the promptness
                 That such a knowledge gives –
                 If anything that lives
                 That is able to know it, knows
                 A better happiness
                 In his dog's life than this,
                 He is welcome to it; most,
                 I apprehend, know less.

Skelpick

sub galea pastor iunctis pice cantat avenis,
proque lupo pavidae bella verentur oves
                                        (Ovid, Tristia)

Below us all day, a mile away, in a flashing
Bend of the river a manikin is for manly
Sport not sustenance casting after and gaffing
The innocent salmon while over us all the clouds
Choir the incessant the variously lovely
Descants of shadows up and across the valley.

This is their glen, the Mackays of Strathnaver who
Were Hanoverian in the '45, who
Furnished the thin red line at Balaclava,
Whose sole exploit in earlier centuries was,
On a tribal foray against the Morays of Dornoch,
The spoliation of Scotland's prime cathedral.

Our childish companion, thinking excrement
Though it be of sheep is hilarious, is shouting
With laughter at me as I kick away sheep-shit
From the green knoll our rented cottage stands on,
Grease on the toe of my boot, me silently cursing
The mindless machines that they are, cropping and cropping.

Yet this is the one who, heaving himself from the small
Citroen he has required should stop, Good Shepherd
Labouring stiff-legged, cradles a possibly crippled
And certainly dam-spurned lamb, and then transports what
If it survives, survives only for slaughter
To a more sheltered dimple in the bracken.

One is not – I hope one is not – escaping the blood
Of the lamb, the excrement, the unsteady gait
After the dug that is always withdrawn, or the holy
Gaffed and gasping fish, the stinking fishwife
Raped beside the Dornoch Firth, by calling
For air, for air, for a distance, calling on

Tristia, the threads of a destiny woven
From a black fleece when a poet was born in Sulmona;
Tristia, the pipe pitch-bonded played
From under a war-bonnet over the shuddering flock;
Tristia, the beldam black Chaldeans'
Disastrous flocking torrent through the birch-trees.

Penelope

And so, the retraction.
Time for it: after much
Effusion, undertow.

And all right, so;
The year wears, and the worn
Capacities, coarsening,

Honour the thing
Beyond them, the transaction
Clinched lately, clinched no more.

Charity for
A while; then, grace withdrawn;
The flow, and then the ebb.

What wove the web
Now frays it, with as much
Devotion in each breath.

Long-absent Death
Veers in the offing; nears
And goes off, to-and-fro.

And all right, so;
This being out of touch
Alone tests constancy.

It is to be
A prey to hopes and fears;
Fears mostly, as is right.

In landfall light
The faithless absentee,
Death, assays our loves.

Though nothing removes
The weight of it, when the year's
Circuit spells: 'dry',

Not asking why
But blessing it, is to see
At last impunity.

The Fountain of Cyanë

I

Her father's brother rapes her!
                    In the bright
Ovidian colours all is for delight,
The inadmissible minglings are recounted
With such finesse: the beery ram that mounted
His niece and, hissing 'Belt up', had her, is
Hell's grizzly monarch gaunt in tapestries;
The thrashing pallid skivvy under him
A vegetation myth; the stinking slum
Is Enna's field where Phoebus ne'er invades
The tufted fences, nor offends the shades;
And her guffawing Ma assumes the land,
Coarsely divine, cacophonous, gin in hand.
Sky-blue, dark-blue, sea-green, cerulean dyes
Dye into fables what we hoped were lies
And feared were truths. A happy turn, a word,
Says they are both, and nothing untoward.
Coloured by rhetoric, to die of grief
Becomes as graceful as a falling leaf;
No chokings, retchings, not the same as dying
Starved and worn out because you can't stop crying.
Cyanë's fable, that one; how she wept
Herself away, shocked for her girl-friend raped –
'Her varied members to a fluid melt,
A pliant softness in her bones is felt . . .'
Sweet lapse, sweet lapse . . . 'till only now remains
Within the channel of her purple veins
A silver liquor . . .' Ah, the master's touch
So suave, mere word-play, that can do so much!
And now at last imperious, in bad taste:
'Nothing to fill love's grasp; her husband chaste
Bathes in that bosom he before embrac'd.'
The spring-fed pool that is Cyanë may
Be visited in Sicily today;

And what's to be made of that? Or how excuse
Our intent loitering outside Syracuse?

II

Modesty, I kept saying,
Temperate, temperate . . . Yes,
The papyrus were swaying
Hardly at all, and late,
Late in the season the rings
Widened upon the reedy
Pool, and the beady-eyed frogs
Volleyed out after mayfly.

Fountain? No jet, no spume,
Spew nor spurt . . . Was this
Where Pluto's chariot hurtled
Up out of 'gloomy Dis'?
Male contumely for that
First most seminal rape,
Proserpine's, prescribes
Some more vertiginous landscape.

Late, late in that season . . .
Easy, easy the lap
And rustle of blue waters . . .
Wholly a female occasion
This, as Demeter launches
One fish in a silver arc
To signalise her daughter's
Re-entry to the dark.

III

The balked, the aborted vision
Permits of the greater finesse;
The achieved one is fugitive, slighter,
One might almost say, 'loose'.

And yet the oceanic
Swells of an unencumbered
Metric jiggle the planes
Epiphanies must glow from.

So, though one might almost say 'loose',
One mustn't. They like the closed-off
Precincts all right, but never
When those exult in their closures.

The shrine is enclosed from the bare
Fields and, three miles away
Clearly in sight, the high-rise
Shimmering haze of the city.

But the fence is of wire; the warped
Palings give easy access;
No turnstile; and at the pool
Of Cyanë, nothing to pay;

No veil to be rent, no grille,
No holy of holies. The Greek
World, one is made to remember,
Was Christianised quite early.

Epiphanies all around us
Always perhaps. And some
Who missed the flash of a fin
Were keeping their eyes on rhyme-schemes.

IV

And so with stanzas . . . moving
From room to room is a habit adapted to winter,
Warm and warming, worship Sunday by Sunday,
And one is glad of it. But when
Now and again I turn the knob and enter
The special chill where my precarious Springs
Hang water-beaded in still air, I hear
A voice announce: 'And this is the
Conservatory!' Greenish misted panes
Of mystifying memory conserve
In an unnatural silence nymph and pool;
It is an outside room, at the end of a range of rooms
But still a room, accounted for or even
Entered upon the impatient plans in my
Infidel youth. At that time no
Nymph, and no pool: still, it appears,
Room left for them – and yet
Rooms should have an outside door, I think;
I wilt for lack of it, though my plants do not.

V

      Yet there was enough in this –
And it was nothing, nothing at all
      'Happened' – enough in this
      Non-happening to cap
      What Scripture says of the Fall

      Which, though it equally may
Not in that sense have happened, is
      A postulate day by day
      Called for, to explain
      Our joys, our miseries.

A fish jumped, silver; small
Frogs took the mayfly; papyrus
   In the Sicilian fall
   Of the leaf was bowing. How
   That weightless weighed with us!

   Why, when an unheard air
Stirred in the fronds, did we assume
   An occidental care
   For proximate cause? Egyptian
   Stems abased their plume.

   So inattentive we are
We think ourselves unfallen. This
   Pool, when Pluto's car
   Whirled up, was wept by Cyanë
   For her abducted mistress.

   One could go round and round
This single and Sicilian less
   Than happening, and ground
   Therein what might suffuse
   Our lives with happiness.

The Thirty-ninth Psalm, Adapted

I said to myself: 'That's enough.
Your life-style is no model.
Keep quiet about it, and while
you're about it, be less overt.'

I held my tongue, I said nothing;
no, not comfortable words.
'Writing-block', it's called;
very discomfiting.

Not that I had no feelings.
I was in a fever.
And while I seethed,
abruptly I found myself speaking:

'Lord, let me know my end,
and how long I have to live;
let me be sure
how long I have to live.

One-finger you poured me;
what does it matter to you
to know my age last birthday?
Nobody's life has purpose.

Something is casting a shadow
on everything we do;
and in that shadow nothing,
nothing at all, comes true.

(We make a million, maybe;
and who, not nobody but
who, gets to enjoy it?)

Now, what's left to be hoped for?
Hope has to be fixed on you.
Excuse me my comforting words
in a tabloid column for crazies.

I held my tongue, and also
I discontinued my journals.
(They accumulated; who
in any event would read them?)

Now give me a chance. I am
burned up enough at your pleasure.
It is all very well, we deserve it.
But shelved, not even with mothballs?

Hear my prayer, O Lord,
and please to consider my calling:
it commits me to squawking
and running off at the mouth.'

Attar of Roses

The mind (the soul) is not
a ghost in the box of the body or brain, although it
excusably seems so. For instance at times
recalling our priests who instructed us in
The Resurrection of the Body

– at Judgement Day, the cadavers out of their coffins,
boxes emerging from boxes! What nonsense,
he blindingly observed –

who was himself, it may be said, a little
fleshy, more than a little coarse,
and maladroit with it, not to say uncivil.

What female parishioner wants him resurrected,
if so in what shape, and for what fanciful purpose?
But all the same, do we live in a nest of boxes,
the nubs of ourselves, so tiny, secreted in
the innermost, most reclusive, most
cramped of the boxes? If not

we have to believe in, we already believe in,
the resurrection of the body

which is not a box, but a main
sweet-smelling part of what the box encloses.

Zion

Mired in it! Stuck in the various
rust-coloured, dove-coloured, yellowish
or speckled muds of history, you mistook
clarity, the dayspring from on high,
for a satisfaction of art, or the condition
of addressing the untutored.

                              (As you never
did, they were otherwise tutored.)

Once, stuck in the mud by the Capitol,
you thought of the ninth buried city,
Richmond, Montgomery, what you had built them for,

of Troy, and of Rome, of Richmond, of Rome, not Zion;

of Troy, of Troynovant, of London,
the West Country, sometimes Geneva,
never of Zion;

of New Caledonia, New
Amsterdam, New Zealand,
Rome (Georgia), other Romes
and Athenses of the North;

New Delhi, Athens, Syracuse, not Zion.

Tutored in computer-processing,
still they may learn of Zion.

Trained in marketing techniques they
may discern in that murk the clarity
of a city not built on seven hills,

not guarding a river-crossing
nor plugging a gap in the mountains.

Unskilled in Islamic culture, they
may still make a Mecca of Zion.

Having heard or not heard of Lindisfarne, Iona,
are not the lot of us pilgrims?

The variegation of muds,
the iridescences,
constitute for some
in youth a passion,
in age a distraction from boredom

which, if designedly aimless
for long enough, merits the name of
Zion or some say Eden.

Their Rectitude Their Beauty

'The angels rejoice in
the excellencies of God;
the inferior creatures in
His goodness; sinners only
in His forgiveness.'

His polar oppositions;
the habitable zones,
His clemencies; and
His smiling divagations,
uncovenanted mercies,

who turned the hard rock into a standing water
and the flint-stone into a springing well.

The voice of joy and health is in the dwellings of the
        righteous;
my eyes are running with rheum
from looking for that health

in one who has stuck by
His testimonies;
who has delighted in
His regimen; who has run
the circuit of His requirements;
whose songs in the caravanserai
have been about His statutes,

not to deserve nor observe them
(having done neither) but
for the angelic reason:

their rectitude,
their beauty.

Saw I Never The Righteous Forsaken

I have been young, and now am old:

but I never saw Mr Worth
denied all reputation,
nor Mrs Worth and the children
go begging in the long run.

Reputations have
what seems when you get to my age
a shortish innings at best.
Remember the champion jockeys?
How many? From how far back?

'He shall bring forth thy
righteousness as the light,
thy judgement as the noonday.'

Banking on posterity
is an unwise investment.
Cold comfort, the little Worths!
Perpetual false dawn!

But merit is ascertainable as daylight;
unarguable justice follows
as certainly as noon ensues from dawn.

Gripping Serial

Man fought against beasts, and won;
Man fought against priests, and won;
Man fought against kings, and won;
Now he fights the Collective.

This drivel is still believed.

Man fought against beasts;
Man fought against Man, and still does;

And there's the end of the series.

Being Angry With God

'Anger, yes. But God is God,'
the impious Pakistani
explained to V.S. Naipaul.
'God is not like people.'

Profound: God is not like people.

Shallow: He ought to be.

Indifference, if you can
manage it (youth can),
disposes of God well enough.

Imran runs up to bowl. The Rajput palaces
live not as art but as the youth
Imran, accelerating, is on the verge of losing.

Even with people, what did
anger ever dispose of?
It ties you in, like love.

Thanks to an undevout Muslim,
we recognise anger with God is
one more way to own Him.

The ex-Christian exclaims:
'But my angers amount to something!'
It is not at all clear that they do,

as Imran Khan
turns and begins his run:
poetry in motion.

The motion is unforgiving;
so is the poetry; so
(unless it is tempered) the Judgement.

Black Hoyden

Mary Jane, she's after me,
Mary Jane, black hoyden.
'Touch of the tar, lad,' says my dad,
'Kitts Nevis or Tahiti.'

Mary Jane has been betrayed.
Don't meddle with Black Hoyden.
'Black eyes like that,' my father said,
'Would scythe a feller's garden.'

Black Hoyden's coming down the hill,
The sleet beginning to fall.
It wavers through the wintry air,
She wavers not at all.

Black Hoyden homing from the mill,
Black Hoyden, Black Hoyden.
Black honour coming tall and still,
A knife in her shawl.

Who is that knife for, Mary Jane?
But I know well, and I know why.
Black eyes lovingly have flashed;
This flash will leave a stain.

Harridan, black hoyden!

Hermes and Mr Shaw

The narrow backyard garden
    Of Mr and Mrs Shaw
Ran between us and, in its cutting, the railway;
    Ran right to left across the end of our,
Our and our neighbours', slightly more ample gardens.

Quite young, a childless couple,
    Mr and Mrs Shaw kept
Themselves to themselves; and so it was no light matter
    When a ball had sailed over the fence, to
Go round and ask to retrieve it.

A minor clerk or else an artisan (I
    Never knew, I imagine), Mr Shaw
Kept mostly a kitchen-garden, though
    Next to his house a patch of lawn
Was where a mis-hit cricket-ball mostly pitched.

The grass there was of a deep, an Irish green,
    And not cropped close. I think it was grown from seed
Not sods. I have the impression lawns
    Grown from seed were thought to be second-rate
As most things were about Mr and Mrs Shaw.

Once, vividly, I saw from my upstairs bedroom
    A flock of white doves dense on that patch of grass
And in the midst of them, accusingly
    And neatly side by side, a pair of my
Canvas shoes, in the dream called quaintly 'plimsolls'.

And dreams – is it not so? – dreams are insistently verbal;
    Vocabulary is the key to them.
Not that I can, or care to, unlock this one:
    What did it guiltily mean, for things of mine
To show up there? Why shoes? Why a snow of doves?

Unlocking dreams is someone else's business.
    What comforts me is that in, say,
1934, as the *kristallnacht* splintered in
    Germany, or soon would, as Stalin moved
Elated to his Great Terror, dramas were

Enacted in my obscure pacific boyhood.
    For was it not that, my dream undeniably proved?
Mr and Mrs Shaw are almost certainly dead.
    Their thin grass, they should know, once took the tread
Of what? Winged sandals? Settle for that: winged sandals.

C. H. Sisson

SELECTED POEMS

Contents

In Time of Famine: Bengal

I do not say this child
This child with grey mud
Plastering her rounded body
I do not say this child
For she walks poised and happy
But I say this
Who looks in at the carriage window
Her eyes are big
Too big
Her hair is touzled and her mouth is doubtful
And I say this
Who lies with open eyes upon the pavement
Can you hurt her?
Tread on those frightened eyes
Why should it frighten her to die?
This is a fault
This is a fault in which I have a part.

A Duckling

I almost prayed for its departing
The tiny bird with sodden feathers
The Christian faith forbids such pity

The duckling weaker than her sisters
Crouching in straw within the hen-coop
Recedes from the immeasurable time.

So small a life with beady eye
Comfort cannot come at and none accompany
Entering among threshed ears the darkening shades.

Stockholm

The dissipated lauds
Of crowds on a glad morning
They have cast clouts
And their skins are a little nearer the sun
Men ordinarily wrapt in care
Feel themselves closer to the off-the-shoulder girls.

And in the church
Clear Nordic voices
        Allena Gud
Under twelve candles and a gold pulpit
Like birds singing
            Tense
Himmelrik
           tillhöra
In narrow pews.

On the Way Home

Like questing hounds
The lechers run through London
From all the alley-ways
Into all the thoroughfares

Until, shoulder to shoulder, they vanish
Into the main line stations
Or the Underground traps them.

A moment of promiscuity at nightfall
Their feet go homewards but their attentions
Are on the nape of a neck or the cut of a thigh
Almost any woman

As Schopenhauer noted
Being more interesting to them than those
Who made their beds that morning.

Victoria Station

The man with nothing to say
May walk in a crowd
His assumed occasions
Will give him reason.

Those therefore whose tacit purposes
Do not allow of apology
Accept the plausible context
Of Victoria Station.

And my verse
Sidles like a child between categories
Instead of poetry I have
Only a location.

The Art of Living

The child can grow
Only by being blind
He owes his greatness
To his fumbling.

The mind askew
From the appetite that drives him
The youth gives reasons
And has destinations.

The old man's waltzing nerves
Misdirect his hand
Aphasia, medicine, hope
Obscure his end.

At an International Conference

These are not words
In which a heart is expressed
You cannot catch in their rhythm
Which way the nerves twist.

This is not the lean orator
With palm touching the sky
It is not the beggar
Defining what is due.

This is not the actor
With tragic or comic mask
Nor the astringent Terpsichore
With whips for muscles.

This is the pot-bellied bankrupt
Naked upon the stage
With a porridge of news-talk
Obscuring his grimace.

Heroes

The heroism of the hunter
Is in his prey, is in his prey
The leaping animal
Always ahead of him.

The heroism of the fisher
Is in his catch, is in his catch
Which he examines
Like snot in his handkerchief.

The heroism of the aviator
Falling through space is the
        fall through space
A little moist jelly
Under a barrow.

The London Zoo

From one of the cages on the periphery
He is brought to London, but only for duty.
As if radio-controlled he comes without a keeper,
Without any resistance, five times in the week.
See him as he rises in his ordered household,
Docile each morning before he is expelled,
Take his bath when he is told, use the right towel,
Reliable as an ant, meticulous as an owl.
His wife, until he is gone, is anxiously protective
In case after all one morning he should resist,
But all is well each day, he hasn't the spirit
– He is edged out of the door without even a murmur.
The road to the station is reassuring
For other black hats are doing the same thing
Some striding blithely who were never athletic,
Others, who were, now encased in Cadillacs,
Snug and still belching from their breakfast bacon,
All, halt and well, keen to be on the train.

Each sits by other whom a long acquaintance
Has made familiar as a chronic complaint,
Although the carapaces they wear are so thick
That the tender souls inside are far to seek.
First there is *The Times* newspaper, held before the eyes
As an outer defence and a guarantee of propriety,
Then the clothes which are not entirely uniform
So as to give the appearance of a personal epidermis,
But most resistant of all is the layer of language
Swathed around their senses like a mile of bandage;
Almost nothing gets in through that, but when something does,
The answering thought squelches out like pus.

These are agreeable companions. At this hour
The people travelling are certainly superior
To those you would have the misfortune to see

If you came up one morning by the eight fifteen
– Typists and secretaries talkative and amorous
With breasts like pears plopping out of their bodices.
Mr Axeter's companions do not distract him:
Carefully he spreads out his copy of *The Times*,
Not unwilling to be stimulated by disasters
Less likely to happen to him than sex,
Disappointed when he finds so boring a centre page
That this morning his mind is not going to be raped.
As an alternative he begins to eavesdrop
On the holidays and car which a lot
Of people have larger and more expensive than he does.
He computes their incomes and their intelligences,
The one larger, the other smaller than his own,
Though his intelligence has shrunk and his income grown
– A not unsatisfactory bit of co-ordination
Which comforts him as his train enters the terminal station.

Out on the platform like money from a cashier's shovel
The responsible people fall at the end of their travel.
Some are indignant that their well-known faces
Are not accepted instead of railway passes;
Others faithfully produce the card by which the authorities
Regulate the movement of animals in great cities.
With growing consciousness of important function
Each man sets out for where he is admired most,
The one room in London where everything is arranged
To enlarge his importance and deaden his senses.
The secretary who awaits him has corrected her bosom;
His papers are in the disorder he has chosen.
Anxieties enough to blot out consciousness
Are waiting satisfactorily upon his desk.

Mr Axeter's office is designed theologically;
Upstairs there is one greater than he;
Downstairs there are several he must keep in submission
Who smoothly profess they are doing what should be done.

Yet the conflict here is no simplified battle,
As you might think, between God and the Devil.
Swords go ping on helmets in every direction
– It is not the fault of God if there is not confusion.
Every man may speak according to his conscience
If he has had it regulated in advance.
A man who goes out to meet a bullet
Is after all some sort of serious character,
For it is him the bullet goes through all right, though he wishes
For an MC or a *Croix de Guerre* or loves spit and polish,
But the man who makes money or who gives wise counsel
Is prostitute or pimp to more live originals
– Still, this is what he takes his money for;
He wouldn't be more honest if he were less of a whore.

Meanwhile from the same train Professor Tortilus
Has gone where they allow him to profess.
Already his zealous students are reading their comics
In the library of the School of Economics
– Judicious journals where those who think thoughts
For a living lay out their unappetising corpses.
The long-haired, the beautiful and the black
And those whose only distinction is to be ignorant
Learn that to be intelligent is to be dull
And that to be perfect you should be statistical as well.
To these hopefuls Professor Tortilus
Will explain the maxims of his own mysterious
Speciality which is nothing less than the complete science
Of correctly conducting human government.
The morning papers, which to many brought only diversion,
To him brought irrefutable demonstration
That all who exercise power will certainly fail
Simply through not following his principles.
All round the School is utter confusion
– The city, Whitehall, industry in ruins –
Only Professor Tortilus, as in a calm season
Still swimming happily in a pool of reason.

There are many others, of course, in the same trainload
As Mr Axeter and Professor Tortilus.
Each has his pretensions and his importance,
Worth good money at the price of utter dependence.
The happiest are convinced by their own rackets,
And there is no racket that does not provide a pretext
For those who are willing to be convinced: one
Incidentally produces something useful as well as money;
Another can be shown, although itself despicable,
To prevent what can be thought of as a worse evil.
Each actor thinks of the particular part he acts
As producing only beneficial effects;
He does harm and picks up his money as unobtrusively
As a physician taking a tip or a waiter a fee.
This lawyer, a vehement defender of the rich against the poor,
Pays no attention to that part of his behaviour,
But advertises himself as a kind of John Hampden
As, without risk to himself, he becomes eloquent
On the alterable right of the poorest he
That is in England to have an advocate, for a fee
To be paid for by the public out of those taxes
The evasion of which is the object of his main practice.
Many who, in a more rational system,
Would be thought mad if they behaved as they do in this one
Are obsessed by the more insidious forms of property:
They buy and sell merchandise they will never see,
Hawking among Wren's churches, and, if they say their prayers,
Say them, without a doubt, to stocks and shares.
– One can barely imagine what scandal would be caused
If they were to be found on their knees in Saint Paul's.
For everything is turned from its right use, so that
Even the lobster that climbs on the business man's plate
Is there less for its colour or its marine taste
Than to impress a customer, or conclude a bargain
– A species of harlotry in edible materials
As the tax-free limousine is a harlot on wheels.

And who am I, you may ask, thus to belly-ache
At my betters? I tell you, I am one of the same lot
– Without lobster and limousine, but, like the rest,
Expending my best energies on the second-best.
There are those who do not, who accept no pay
For work they know would better be done otherwise
– Not the scabs of culture for whom any talk of the arts
Brings money to their purses and a throb to their silly hearts,
But the few still remaining who have decided to live
Without taking account of what is remunerative.
You will hardly believe it, but it is those few
Who are the only spectators in this zoo
– And yet to call it a zoo is certainly an injustice
To the family of hyenas, apes and bustards
Who have no difficulty in speaking with their own voice
And do not look to be respected for their price.
It is rather as a somewhat extravagant machine
That the managerial classes should be seen,
Whose only animal activity is when
Mr Cog returns at the end of the day to his hen.

Adam and Eve

They must be shown as about to taste of the tree.
If they had already done so they would be like us;
If they were not about to do so they would be
Not our first parents but monsters.

You must show that they were the first who contrived
An act which has since become common,
With head held high when it is conceived
And, when it is repented of, dangling.

There must be not one Adam but two,
The second nailed upon the tree:
He came down in order to go up
Although he hangs so limply.

The first Adam, you will recall, gave birth
To a woman out of his side;
For the second the process was reversed
And that one was without pride.

By the Lift Gate

Well I can understand your contraction
The lines by your eyes and your pointed nose:
You pull your coat about you (but I can guess)
Advancing one foot with suspended toes.

The melancholy at the approach of winter
Is not for the season but the summer lost,
Your juices retracted, but not yet gone
The moment, you would probably say, passed.

But whether you reached for that moment
And so fell headlong into the abyss
Or waited on the brink, all is one in the end:
You are approaching forty and no peace.

I have hunted your eyes like weasels among the ferns:
Who can say when there is an end of hope
Or what peace there would have been in satisfaction?
Close the lift gate and go up on the end of a rope.

Grandmother

Grandmother wheeling a perambulator
With outstretched arms and senescent leer,
What reason for hope have you here?
Shame on the body at fourscore!

Only Christ can have mercy on you now;
You can look for none from Venus or Lucina.
The boy's stout finger admonishes you
What a danger to women he intends to be.

Turn up the pram and let him tumble upon
The flat silk front that covers your dugs.
You are glad to feel the strength of his legs;
He is harmless in your lap as others were not.

Once you gave your body to the poor.
That will sustain you now more than any prudence.
Now you may give it to this young impotent
As he laughs and kicks but you know more.

Grandmother you may perambulate
With broken spokes and distorted frame;
You are cheerful and it may be half crazed
Not for what you have but for what you gave.

The Temple

Who are they talking to in the big temple?
If there were a reply it would be a conversation:
It is because there is none that they are fascinated.
What does not reply is the answer to prayer.

Eclogue

CORYDON, DAPHNIS

Put the buggers under the wall.
No-one will notice that you have strangled the bastards.
Thus Corydon, regardful of his flock.
Daphnis took a bunch of *parfum chèvre*
In his great mit and, having adjusted his jock-strap,
Set out to dazzle or woo the incomparable Chloe.
I suppose she was lying on her back
With legs wide open, pretending to snore.
At any rate Daphnis made short work of her.
Back with his mates, Corydon took up the pipe:
All things were made for the violent and the greedy.
Thank you, Pan, for your inclination towards us.

STREPHON, DORINDA

STREPHON: So, Dorinda, you will not take my garland
Although I am an educated shepherd;
I pipe all day but you cannot hear me.
DORINDA: Too apt a replica of human life
Is apt to distress those for whom it is intended.
STREPHON: You know a trick better than distress;
You sit all day with your knees hunched,
Your mind concentrated on counting your lambs.
If you took our country pleasures
You might suddenly become endowed with understanding.
DORINDA: That is a fantasy of the adolescent
And really only a pun on carnal knowledge.
The shepherd who seeks to move me with his pipe
Does not thereby acquire a right to my conversation.
STREPHON: But if the understanding is not carnal
It is no more than your tallies without your sheep.

DORINDA: Do not press me to accept that argument.
I will bathe myself in the clear stream
But do not join me, Strephon.

DORINDA, DAPHNIS, CORYDON

DAPHNIS: Hey, Corry, that tart is taking her clothes off.
CORYDON: Leave her; she don't need no help from you.
DAPHNIS: Watch me. Daphnis is the boy for this.
DORINDA: Daphnis, you are deceived by your own name.
DAPHNIS: I never heard a tart who spoke like that before.
DORINDA: Which of your two tongues is the more eloquent
I have, I assure you, not the slightest doubt.
Even with a voice of full-throated melody
It is hard enough to say what is being expressed,
A fortiori with a tongue which merely licks.
DAPHNIS: Lie down over there and I will show you.
If Strephon can't manage you well then I can.
DORINDA: It is not in the management but in what is
    managed
Or rather in whether what is distinguished from who
That the problem lies
And if that is the limit of your invention
You will really get us no nearer a solution.
Corydon, taking his pipe, induced this song:
Charm without thinking, calf-deep in the splashing water
Under the green shadow that makes your flesh a thought.

DAPHNIS, STREPHON

DAPHNIS: Shepherds without identity is a good lark
— Dorinda and me copulating like flies.
To be nothing but an objective buzz!
STREPHON: For you that is a comprehensible ambition
Because you are not aware that being an object
Is different in kind from observing what is.
Even the pleasure you took with Chloe,

Vigorous and unreflective though it was,
Did not succeed in reaching annihilation
Nor can you forget her foul breath
Or the way her teeth met you.
DAPHNIS: Chloe was all right though she stank a bit
But what I should like is to get Dorinda
When she has stopped being a naiad.
STREPHON: Corydon's song was meant to warn you against
    that
As much as to silence Dorinda.
It was only an echo from the philosophers
Came through her lips and reverberated through the grotto
And philosophy is harmless enough.
But for you to suppose you could achieve brutality
And become like a May-bug driven against a pane
By uniting yourself with one so rational
Is to misunderstand the nature of love.

DAPHNIS, STREPHON, DORINDA

DORINDA: Indeed it is the nature of love which is in question
But why either of you should think he can be united
Merely by favour of a ridiculous pipe
With someone conceived of as an entity
Of a different kind, is more than I can say.
STREPHON: Dorinda, you are a monster of vanity.
You understand well enough that the problem
Is not the penetration of your superb self
But how we come to be talking of it.
If you in fact had been that slight figure,
More gracious than I can say, among the rushes
I need have been no more than my eyes.
It was in that moment Corydon made his song.
That was no sooner ended, however, than this lout
Daphnis, forever with his mind on the bacon,
Comes up with his unremunerative plans for action

And you quickly lay claim to an identity
Which means you must not be touched.

DAPHNIS, STREPHON, DORINDA, CORYDON

CORYDON: My verse also was a deception.
It is time we came to the sheep-shearing.
Here, Daphnis, take hold of this crook.
Go and collect the flock from the long meadow.
Strephon, you get the antiseptic shears
And grind them on the stone behind the dairy.
I will look after Dorinda.

DORINDA, CORYDON

CORYDON: Put on your clothes and come and eat a posset
Of curds and whey under the great oak.
Perhaps you would care to be my secretary;
I need a girl with brains to count my sheep.
DORINDA: Well, that would certainly be better than love;
I am rather fed up with being admired.
I should like instead to be useful.
CORYDON: You could be doubly so if you came with me.
I have employment enough for your intelligence
And at night, when we have counted our money,
We will play at natural objects.
DORINDA: I cannot too much praise your invention.
Midas was embarrassed by his golden touch
But you turn gold to nature.
CORYDON: So that is fixed?
DORINDA: I will accept you if you make it legal.

DAPHNIS, STREPHON, CORYDON, DORINDA

DAPHNIS AND STREPHON: Everything is ready for the
sheep-shearing.
DORINDA: Boys, I shall enjoy watching you work.

To Brian Higgins on First Reading
Notes While Travelling

I could not understand your book
Although I had read some poems before,
So I tried holding it upside down
And read it sitting on the floor.

This worked marvellously, at first
I received several bizarre impressions.
It was a good laugh, and that is something
For a man in my position.

Then I noticed that while I was reading
You were working on the floor below.
If that is his game, I said to myself,
I'm damned if I will follow!

So I turned the book the right way up
And read it by the light of reason.
Damn this fellow, I said,
Who thinks he can live under his own legislation!

Damn that for a cock-eyed idea
– Doing away with civil servants!
Someone has to hold up the post
For Brian Higgins to lean upon.

What a Piece of Work is Man

The man of quality is not quite what he was
In the days when that was a technical term
But there are, happily, a number of qualities
You can be a man of, and it is hard if there is not one
In which you can claim distinction.
Like speaks only to like, and without quality
Which you cannot communicate because you have it by blood
Or some subtler misfortune known as intelligence
There can be no speech.
It is by quality that you are not alone.
Those gathered around the bar, as they lift their beer-mugs
Tremble to break the enchantment of what is common:
It is so by the well or the dhobi-ghat
Or the club where charm may not exceed a pattern.
Pray do not address me in Japanese
In which language my hopes express themselves ill.
Yet what I have in common with the cat
Suffices for a very short conversation
Each time we meet.

Love is of opposites, they say: but the opposite
Is by way of being a philosophical refinement
And what wedges itself in the female slot
Though apposite enough, is hardly that.
If what goes on there is understanding
Then understanding is something different.
Do not imagine the body cannot lie;
What else have we for lying or for truth?
We talk by species and genus.
God who created us made himself understood
First in the thunder, then in the cloud and then in us.
I wish I did not hear him in the thunder.

How does it happen that the table leg
Has this curve in one age, that in another?

Or that the carved figures of men
Differ more than the men themselves?
Conception rules the art.
How then can one man speak to another?

Is it not the conception
Past any man's thinking, that is expressed
Even in the voice that seems to speak clearly?
And in the million voices that chatter together
Over this peninsula or that continent
A peculiar god looms
And what seems to be said between two people
Is only part of a complex conversation
Which they cannot hear and could not understand.
Yet it is only by taking part in that conversation
That they can give names to their own movements.
I lift my hand: there is a hand, certainly.
I touch your cheek: a hand touches a cheek.
In the name of what god? I have no name of my own.
Can I see my own movement except in conception?
What art has the heart, how does it understand
Its own beat?
The heart opened and the body chilled
Or the mind unneeded because the body is perfect.
The leaves of the jungle are parted. There comes out
One who moves like a deer.
And in the city the tapes record the prices,
Which is also a mode of understanding.

Words are not necessary between bodies.
O admirable attempt to forget to be human.
But you are clothed in words
Less of your own devising than your own body
And of which nothing can strip you but death.
Age and forgetfulness may leave you mumbling,
The words eating your toes or soft belly:
How are you speaking now?

From a Train

Two on a railway bank
They do not need their own thoughts
Their organs hanging on the verge.

The hanging gardens of Babylon
Flower in vast space between their legs
They crouch with great knees side by side.

Hands laced across the shoulders O
The light electrical touch of reason
O need they give each other names?

Go home at last to parents' eyes
The spirit unscaling as you go
Unlace those arms and be alone.

What you will not believe as you lie down
And call on God for the fornication you did not dare
Is that by chastity you have begun your age.

This loneliness will become your natural condition
When everything has been added and taken away
You will be left with a small grit which is yourself.

The Shortest Day

How can you tell whether a man is human?
Surely Christ must have mercy on the souls of animals
How else could I know who is my neighbour?

I met a man running across a plain
With taut cheeks and movements like an engine
There is need of mercy for me who encountered him.

Is it arms and legs, the long hands
The armoury of sex and the spoken word
Or what little the premature foetus is born with?

It cannot be only those I can speak to
It is those who are answerable to God
— May I be content not to identify them.

Badger my friend on the periphery of the city
The snow covers the time of the Incarnation
And I cannot understand the hard mind of God.

C. H. SISSON 279

Human Relations

My mind is so evil and unjust
I smile in deprecation when I am flattered
But inside the palace of my smile
Is the grovelling worm that eats its own tail
And concealed under the threshold of my lips
Is the trustless word that will wrong you if it can.
Come nearer to me therefore, my friend,
And be impressed by the truth of my explanation.
No less, lady, take my chaste hand
While the other imaginatively rifles your drawers.

The Queen of Lydia

Candaules, King of Lydia,
Whose mouth was bigger than his prick

Boasted about the Queen his wife:
'You ought to see her in her bath;

She is a smasher.' Gyges said
He thought it inappropriate.

He was a soldier and he knew
The elements of discipline.

He also knew you did not trust
A master with an outsized mouth.

The King insisted, and arranged
Gyges should stand behind the door

While she came in and got undressed.
And this he did. Candaules lay

Discreetly in his double bed,
His nose above the counterpane.

He liked the Queen to take her time
And put her folded garments on

A bench some distance from the bed,
Then strut about the room a bit.

All this she did; and Gyges watched.
Was his mind on his duty then?

He shook as he stood by the door.
As the Queen turned her lovely back

He made a noise and then went out.
Alas, he was not quick enough.

The Queen said nothing; she was sly
And thought instead and went to sleep.

Next day she sent for Gyges and
He trembled as behind the door.

She gave him this alternative:
'One of you two goes to the pot.

Either you kill the shameless king
And lie beside me in his bed

And also govern Lydia
Or I will have him murder you.'

The choice was easy: no one dies
Rather than sleep beside a girl.

And the Queen's motive? She believed
(The Lydians are barbarians)

To be seen naked was a shame
Which only death could expiate

Or marriage, as in Gyges' case.
So you see how barbarians are.

Eurydice

If I took your maidenhead
As I well might do,
Softly to Acheron
I would go down.
Parting the rushes there:
'Where are the King and Queen
Of this fell kingdom? Has
Love any part in it?'
Striking the lyre,
Orpheus in every inch.
'If the legend is true
It has some part. Proserpine
Was fetched here from the fields,
April bore her in love.
This reign, so long,
Over the bloodless dead
Began with love.'
And the King with pity:
'You shall have her if you can
And not look back.'
Softly, past the sedge,
I drew back. Eurydice!
Faint words come from you.
When you stretch your hand
It is hardly air you catch,
One voice between us
Hangs and is lost.
Eurydice!
Retracted now. The gates.
Seven days beside the Styx
Orpheus sat, without corn
Wine of any country
No food but tears.
Within the gates of the dead
Eurydice. Weeping,

If there can be tears.
Orpheus goes back to Thrace,
In those hard mountains
Learns to hate all women.
For her, it might be said
But that is false.

The Shape

The passions are the shape of man.
I put it on a drawing board.

Show the integument drawn back.
Draw pity round about the heart.

Pity is small and avarice
No bigger, where the nostrils curl

But envy goes from top to toe
And lust runs from the radial point

Into the tip of every limb
And every hair upon the head

And sorrow blackens out the lines
Of every hope; and deep despair

Gathers like bile above the groin
Until it fills the abdomen.

Lucky the shape was sketched before
I drew back the integument.

The Affirmative

The trick of sex, there is no doubt,
First taught the animals to speak.

But Yes is not a word at all;
The first word that they spoke was No.

All conversation still remains
A gloss upon the negative.

For Yes could only hold its tongue;
Its work is in another place.

Lines on the Rector's Return

The Devil has become Rector of this parish
And is having a tremendous success.

Every year the collections go up
As up in the pulpit he denounces Charity.

But the subtlest part of his exposition
Is that in which he removes the grounds for Hope

And the part the Devil seems to admire most himself
Is that in which he twists Faith to his own meaning.

Faith, Hope and Charity, these three:
Look out, here comes Mr Haggerty.

Metamorphoses

I

Actaeon was a foolish hind
To run from what he had not seen.

He was a hunter, and had called
An end to slaughter for that day

And laid his weapons by a well.
Diana knew the man he was

But took her kirtle from her waist.
She gave her arrows to her maids

Then dropped her short and flimsy dress.
There was some muscle on the girl.

I think she knew the hunt was up
But set the hounds upon the man

To show her bitter virgin spite.
There was some blood but not her own.

Actaeon sped, his friends hallo'ed,
The forest rang but not with tears.

His favourite whippet bit his flank:
His friends hallo'ed him to the kill

Which they were sure he would enjoy.
Diana by the fountain still

Shuddered like the water on her flesh
And after that there came the night.

II

— Or else he was a rutting stag
Turned to a man because he saw

Diana bathing at the pool
— As you might turn a foreskin back.

III

Pygmalion was an artful man;
Sculpsit and pinxit were his trade.

He would not have a woman in
The confines of his silky bed;

The ones he knew were troublesome.
Still, he admired the female form

And cut another in that shape
But it was marble, rather hard.

He laid it down upon his bed
And drew a purple coverlet

Across its shapely breasts and legs.
However, it did not respond.

He got it up and gave it clothes
And brought it several sorts of toys.

It did not speak a single word
So in despair he said his prayers.

He did not even dare to say
'This marble' or 'this ivory';

He merely said he'd like a girl
Resembling one he'd made himself.

After his prayers the boy went home
And got back to his kissing game.

To his surprise the girl grew warm;
He slobbered and she slobbered back

— This is that famous mutual flame.
The worst of all was yet to come.

Although he often wished her back
In silent marble, good and cold

The bitch retained her human heat,
The conquest of a stone by art.

May Venus keep me from all hope
And let me turn my love to stone.

IV

O will you take a fluttering swan
Eurotas, on your plashy banks?

Where the dissimulating bird
Fled from a Venus he had coaxed

Into an eagle with a beak.
Eurotas showed beneath her waves

The rippling image of a girl.
She rose to take the frightened bird

And struggled with him to the bank.
It was the bird came out on top.

Its wings concealed the thing it did
But showed the fluttering legs and hands.

The bird became a stable thing:
There are such dangers for a girl.

Europa felt a sighing bull
Beside her, as she gathered flowers.

It was a gentle, milk-white beast
And tried to graze upon her hair.

She patted and embraced its neck;
Its breath grew deeper as she stroked.

At last she climbed upon his back,
One hand upon a stubby horn.

Over his broad and shaggy cloth
The creature felt the gentle limbs

And in a trice he was away.
Europa held the swimming beast;

She looked at the receding shore
And clutched her garments from the wind.

V

When Virgo crosses with the Ram
Expect a rain of falling stars,

A spilling cornucopia
Betokening plenty, but no peace,

A Danae in her open boat.
The eleemosynary shower

That fell, can now get up again
And it is Easter in the world.

The first age was the age of gold;
The age of iron is our own.

VI

The day, the year, the century,
The glacial winter, and the spring

And then the naked summer brings
The rutting stag to the church door.

But first the Phaeton from the crown
Of heavens descends into the waves.

There was no reason in his course
And on his way he burnt the world

And when you visited the shades
Did you see my Eurydice,

Christ, on that terrifying day?
I sit beneath the pulpit for

The bitter, abnegated hour.
I have no notion what you did.

In manus tuas. Afterwards.
Except you walked three days in hell.

Was there numb kindness in the shades?
Who is that nacreous figure there

The empty sunlight falls upon
Although there is no light to fall?

Will she resume the upper light?
And when you come to Thomas in

The confines of his doubting room
Was she left in an orange-grove?

There was a garden. Calvary.
And Adam fell where you got up.

But was the resurrected flesh
Less tempted than the flesh of Eve?

The naked figure in the grove
Diana's or the risen Christ's?

Her altar or the flesh we eat?
The world is uncreated by

The death of him that made the world.
By the slain lamb there trots the fawn.

VII

Here are two stories of old men:
The virtuous Boaz is the first.

He lay upon the threshing floor
And dreamed of Ruth, who soon came in

And while in sleep he saw the fields
Where she had stooped to gather corn

She gently lifted, in the dark,
The rug that hid his bony toes.

It was a rather pleasant dream.
Benign and virtuous to himself

He wished he could be warm like Ruth.
And there she was. But he was scared.

He sent her home and merely bit
The aged spit upon his beard

And did it honestly next day.
As he was rich the world approved.

The second story is about
Two men whose desiccated years

Were sheltered in the splendid house
Of Joacim, a juicy lord.

They earned their keep by being just
But saw Susanna every day.

She was a soft and tender bit.
They noticed when she took her bath

And both devised a pleasant plan
To help her with the soap and rinse.

They waited in the garden where
She took it when the sun was hot.

Unhappily it warmed them too
And made them lie to get their way.

Then they were frightened, and resumed
Their great pretence of being just.

Less fortunate than Boaz, they
Could only hope to have her killed

But even this did not come off
And Daniel had them cut in two.

VIII

Which otherwise might have been born.
They carried in a bloody tray

This unripe apple plucked within
The forest of the uterus.

This one at least will not arrive
At ages suitable for tears.

Within this forest everything
Begins. Although I may not say

Eurydice walks with her tears
It is the grove where they began.

It is the grove where I walked out,
Blind as upon my latest days.

I had a kind of folded life.
The butterfly with its wet wings

Has twice the power I had to fly.
And how then to the garden where

The loaded Tree of Knowledge stood?
Deceptively completed man

Beside a woman as complete?
No expectation in his eyes

His member like a falling leaf;
The fronded entrance to Eve's cave

Admitting no posterity.
The shining apples had no life.

Then how could Adam come to find
A tree more naked than himself,

Excoriate of leaves and fruit
And he himself nailed to the boughs?

Some serpent must have let him hope,
Which his glazed body could not do

Without hortation from a flesh
He had forgotten was his own.

Some spasm must have found its end
And broken his tumescent heart.

Eve must have let her children out
From her forced womb, to right and left.

But first, within, the spinning wave
Of sperm had sent its foam-flake out

To meet the southward-seeping egg
And this encounter did not hear

Either the paradisal speech
Exchanged when congress was agreed

Or the reared serpent's good advice
So soft that it became a hiss.

It needed Cain and Abel too,
The brothers Murder and Incite

And Noah with his upturned eyes,
Lifting his skirts out of the wet

And Abraham in fear of God,
Getting his holy cutlass out.

The sober, patriarchal life
In which the richest was the best

And now the surgeon with his smile
And sister's deferential cough.

IX

The metamorphosis of all.
Or he was nothing but a child

Magi attended for the star
And shepherds for their singing ears.

Funny how he became a Mass,
To eat his body, when he died,

The first essay of carpentry
Building an ark for the whole world

As you might nail a coffin up.
The golden age began anew;

What had been first became the last.
Declension to the age of iron

Was unimportant after all.
And yet there must remain a doubt.

The giants piling up the sky,
Pelion on Ossa, also rose

And what will rise must also fall.
We know it by experience.

It is the waning of the year.
A death in spring-time is the best.

The State of the Arts

dedicated to The Lord Goodman

36 poets of the London area
Assembled at 105 Piccadilly.
I hope they did not spoil the carpets,
Hawking and spitting all over the place.
The rent is high, explained the curator,
But we were attracted by the situation.
Have you seen our furniture?
I do not know how many pounds per square foot
For the Council Chamber, but then, think of the members,
'Selected for pre-eminence in the Arts'
– A Sunday-paper novelist, and some others.
Into whose hands, Muses, are you fallen?
Presiding over the whole, like a frog,
Mr Wilson's lawyer, 55, unmarried,
Whose career dates from the Labour victory
(See *Who's Who*).

                    Poets, tumble downstairs.
They are marble, and you should be grateful.
There is safety in numbers.

Trafalgar Square

There is no remedy but death
And that you need not hanker for
For no obscure oblivion
Waits for your bones, but certain hope
Of coming to a blinding light,
Each part of you without pity
Remembered. No extreme failure
Not matched with desert; honey,
If it is for you at all, laid on your burns.
This is my belief, hardly to be reconciled
With that demure Saviour I apprehend
Somewhere among the shades. But all is mystery,
In pity of my understanding, not
To wrap myself in, here in Trafalgar Square.

The Usk

Christ is the language which we speak to God
And also God, so that we speak in truth;
He in us, we in him, speaking
To one another, to him, the City of God.

I

Such a fool as I am you had better ignore
Tongue twist, malevolent, fat mouthed
I have no language but that other one
His the Devil's, no mouse I, creeping out of the cheese
With a peaked cap scanning the distance
Looking for truth.
Words when I have them, come out, the Devil
Encouraging, grinning from the other side of the street
And my tears
Streaming, a blubbered face, when I am not laughing
Where in all this
Is calm, measure,
Exactness
The Lord's peace?

II

Nothing is in my own voice because I have not
Any. Nothing in my own name
Here inscribed on water, nothing but flow
A ripple, outwards. Standing beside the Usk
You flow like truth, river, I will get in
Over me, through me perhaps, river let me be crystalline
As I shall not be, shivering upon the bank.
A swan passed. So is it, the surface, sometimes
Benign like a mirror, but not I passing, the bird.

III

Under the bridge, meet reward, the water
Falling in cascades or worse, you devil, for truthfulness
Is no part of the illusion, the clear sky
Is not yours, the water
Falling not yours
Only the sheep
Munching at the river brim
Perhaps

IV

What I had hoped for, the clear line
Tremulous like water but
Clear also to the stones underneath
Has not come that way, for my truth
Was not public enough, nor perhaps true.
Holy Father, Almighty God
Stop me before I speak

– per Christum.

V

Lies on my tongue. Get up and bolt the door
For I am coming not to be believed
The messenger of anything I say.
So I am come, stand in the cold tonight
The servant of the grain upon my tongue,
Beware, I am the man, and let me in.

VI

So speech is treasured, for the things it gives
Which I can not have, for I speak too plain
Yet not so plain as to be understood
It is confusion and a madman's tongue.

Where drops the reason, there is no one by.
Torture my mind: and so swim through the night

As envy cannot touch you, or myself
Sleep comes, and let her, warm at my side, like death.
The Holy Spirit and the Holy One
Of Israel be my guide. So among tombs
Truth may be sought, and found, if we rejoice
With Ham and Shem and Japhet in the dark
The ark rolls onward over a wide sea.
Come sleep, come lightning, comes the dove at last.

Seeming

What the imagination could only imagine
Is, ah how different from the thing done
Which is only a done thing, fine
To the spectator perhaps, but not to me.

It is somebody else's imagination.
Beauty, are you so?
My heart craves for you. Eaten out, hollow
What is this space for then, and how lived in?

Hollow heart also, you have nothing to live for.
It could not be me, for I am nothing at all.
Are you there, certainty, behind that beauty?
Are you there, or what?

Morpheus

Naked people
Stepping, under mackintoshes
Through the dim city

The elect, the dead
The indifferent, head on
Into the underground. Morpheus.

What underneath? Proserpine dances
Exactly with legs, arms curled
About her head like a duster

There are green fields, below
Memory cannot reach, trees discover
Or old tales render probable.

It was a snake, some say
Bit at her ankle. So
I would myself.

It was thorn
Entangled her. I
Could wind about her.

It was the wind
Caught and advanced her flying
Hair. It was tears distresses

Of my hope and finding
Destroyed, unkindly, what hope there was.
That was my failure.

So against the crowd, perfect
I stand like a lamp-post, they flow past me
Stoney eyes, mine or theirs.

In insula Avalonia

I

Huge bodies driven on the shore by sleep
The mountain-woman rocks might fall upon
And in the cavity the heaped-up man.

Sleep on the island like a witty zone
Seas break about it, frolicking like youth
But in the mists are eyes, not dancers, found.

Hurt is the shepherd on the inland hill
He has a cot, a staff and certain sheep
Stones are his bed, his tables and his bread.

This is not where the sirens were, I think
But somewhere, over there, the next approach
Behind that other island in the mist.

That was the song, beyond the linnet-call
At the cliff's edge, below the plunging gull
The fish it found, the enemy or Christ.

II

Counting up all the ways I have been a fool,
In the long night, although the convent clock
Winds several hours around Medusa's locks,

Geryon and Chrysaor are with me now
– Sure there was bad blood in that family –
And yet the worst of all was done by love.

The fool: but not the bow and naked babe
But top-coat murderers with sullen looks
And yet Medusa was a temple harlot.

Under the river-bank a seeping wind
Ripples the bubbles from a passing fish
No colder memory than gloomy Dis.

Look, for you must, upon the fine appearance,
The creature had it and is formless dead.
Now come no nearer than to straws in glass.

III

Dark wind, dark wind that makes the river black
– Two swans upon it are the serpent's eyes –
Wind through the meadows as you twist your heart.

Twisted are trees, especially this oak
Which stands with all its leaves throughout the year;
There is no Autumn for its golden boughs

But Winter always and the lowering sky
That hangs its blanket lower than the earth
Which we are under in this Advent-tide.

Not even ghosts. The banks are desolate
With shallow snow between the matted grass
Home of the dead but there is no one here.

What is a church-bell in this empty time?
The geese come honking in a careless skein
Sliding between the mort plain and the sky.

What augury? Or is there any such?
They pass over the oak and leave me there
Not even choosing, by the serpent's head.

IV

O there are summer riders
On the plain
           in file or two by two

It is a dream

For Winter, one by one, is wringing us
The withers, one, and scrotum-tight the other

Yet I am here
Looking down on the plain, my elbow on
The sill

From which I night by night and day by day
Watch
           for the moon pours swimmingly

Upon this field, this stream
That feeds my sleep.

Be night
Be young
The morning half begun
Palls on the waiting mind and makes it scream

O Minnich, Minnich

Who is the lady there by Arthur's lake?
None is. A willow and a tuft of grass
But over bones it broods, as over mine
Somewhere
Except
         nowhere

Bind up your temples and begone from here
No need to answer. What is there to fear?

Only the wind that soughs, and soughs, and soughs.
Some say it does, and others contradict
Some say sleep strengthens, others that it kills
This music comes

               from Wendover I think
Where meaning is at least, there, sure, am I.

V

Out in the sunlight there I am afraid
For dark depends upon the nascent mind
The light, the envy and the world at large

A field for flood, and fish and such-like deer
The willows standing in between the pools
Great siege this morning, in the morning-time

The water rustles like a turning page
Write then who will, but write upon the stream
Which passes nonchalantly through the hedge

No word of mine will ever reach the sea
For mine and words are clean contrary things
Stop here for envy, go there for your love

For love of persons are the passing geese
Swans on the flood, the dopping water-fowl
The cloud that cumbers while the sky is blue.

Awful at nights, the mind is blue today
Enlarged without a purpose like a lake
For purpose pricks the bubble of our thoughts.

Climb back to sleep, the savage in that mine
Picks with his teeth and leaves his skull to dry
O skull and cross-bones on the earthen floor

My earth, my water, my redundant trees
Breaking the surface like a stitch in skin.
No word but weather, let me be like that.

VI

A ruminant in darkness. So am I
Between the skin and half a hope of hell
Tell me till morning where the savage stops.

His eyes beside the fire. The burning peat
Is quiet, quiet, quiet till it shrieks
Not what the hammer was but what it says

The eyes on Thursday and the mind that waits
For sabbaths of intent but does no thing
Not seeking, waiting for a peaceful end

What wind is in the trees? What water laps
Extravagantly round the seeping hedge?
A house on sticks, where several yearned before

The skin, the furze, the movement into sleep
The watery lids beside the river bank
Mirrors of emptiness, O what way in?

VII

A mine of mind, descend who can that way
As down a staircase to the inner ring
Where figures are at liberty, and play

A plain of ghosts, among the rest a girl
(And none had touched her, though the serpent's teeth
Met in her heel below the flying skirt)

She gathered flowers, exacting from their grace
An outward parallel for grace of skin,
Petals for fingers, petals for arms and legs.

This transient surface is the thing I seek
No more, perhaps, than scale upon the eyes
Do not walk with her, winds are blown that way

A storm of leaves and all may disappear
And yet below the circle of my mind
Playing in spring-time there is Proserpine.

But I am rather Cerberus than Dis
Neither receive nor yet pursue this child
Nor am I Orpheus who could bring her back.

I stand and roar and only shake my chain
The river passes and gives others sleep
I am the jaws nothing will pass between.

VIII

The mind beyond the reach of human time
Mine or another's, let me now perceive
Time has turned sour upon the earth for me

A little earth, walking upon the earth
A molehill, Mother, on your credent slopes
But moving, time against me, everywhere

This is the lump out of which I was made
The hands, the feet, the brain no less is mud
What does not crumble must remain in shape

The shape of man, but moles are better off
Boring the hill-side like a nit in cheese
They asked for blindness, that is what they have

But I for light, for sleep, for anything
Moving my hands across the surfaced world
Exacerbate in darkness, though alive

I never came from any natural thing
To take this shape which is not mine at all
Yet I am I am I and nothing more

If any took this shape I took this shape
Yet taking what I did not ask to have
And being nothing till I took this shape

The shape of shafts of light and falling suns
Meteors incarcerate in balls of mud
A cracked example of a better kind

Admit you came because you could not know
Walk in the garden as you did one day
And if you cannot flatter, answer back.

IX

Some seek examples in the world of sense
They slide across the retina like dreams
Yet are objective in the world of deeps

Which swimmers may attempt, that move all ways
Across the current, from the pebbly floor
Up to the surface where the morning breaks

If any capture what the water-weed
Holds brightly like a bubble on its stem
Or what may disappear in lengthening dark

Volumes of sleep will turn the swimmer's arm
His leg will gently bump the feathered rock
Gulls cry above, sleep has no place for them

A call, a cry, a murder in the street
Is sign of others lonely as yourself
The Lord have mercy, others may as well.

X

I do not know and cannot know indeed
And do not want a word to tell me so
A sentence is construction more than I.

I feel, I vomit. I am left to earth
To trample and be trampled, in my turn
But always rotting from the day I came

Thy kingdom come. And could I pray indeed
I would be höhnisch and destroy the world
This is not what is meant and nor am I.

So let my silence fasten on a rock
Be lichen, that is plenty, for my mind
And not be where I was. Where is he? Gone

The empty space is better than himself
But best of all when, certain winters past,
No one says: There he was, I knew him well.

Dialogue of the Soul and God, or of Psyche with Cupid

I

Love, hear me come
I rustle up the stairs and am with God
Come over me
You winged ecstatic stranger in my bed

I come
Psyche lie in the dawn
And do not turn your head
I may be Christ

I lie
Covered in flowers
Nature's fair canopy, and dream
So must it be

I wing
Across an azure main, far out
The sea is mine
White gulls

Though I lie still, I fly
With you, against the cloud
It cannot be
Yet I am you I know

Ah, take no candle dear
To spoil your dream
I am the edge of things
And will be gone

Will you not love
The resting limbs in bed?
Not I, my dear, the wind
The kami-kaze I.

II

Lord Wind
I am your patience so I am not I

If you were you
I would dissolve
So not in peace

I, I
The entropy of every beast
Sigh out your wind

Dissolve
Be less than nothing now
I hawk

You kestrel on the wing
What wind
Can hold you now?

My police
Is in my eye

My current flows away
Less than the wind

Hawk not

Not I

Descending

I

I rise upon the wind

I, I?

III

No mind has spoken yet

Nor will
You catch-cheat, catch-care face
You foot

I foot
Wandering upon the ground

You badger-track, you walk

Split eye
Half looking up, half down
What shall I do?

Do nothing more, but sleep
Geschwind

IV

This is the end
Of all I ever made

You make?
The makeless maker is the make of you

Down eyes

Down head
And do you feel my foot across the nape?

My hair
Mops up your feet as Mary Magdalen's did

Slut, I am there.

Saint-Rémy

I should have descended, perhaps
The hill
On a May morning
Ma bello is it I can please you?
That can never be.
You have pleased, you have pleased, all the long living
Not a tear from me, I wipe it, in telling
Et les aieuls, grandfathers, grandmothers,
Down the street, in procession.

Tears
Are not always there for the danger of having them
Sometimes they pour out
In pleasure over the thin cascade
Down the steps, from the sacred source
There is no pleasure like that of descending
Hand in hand, plucking the rosemary
Plucking the thyme.

Over this effete cavern the sun

Sets
Down the hillside, walking
Rosemary, this time
At the foot of the cavern where the nymph stood
I did not understand her, not I
The steps descend
There is an underworld, in that water

Black

I intend no evil, come a little nearer, plunge
The water is extremely salt, I did not
Expect this effect
Nor can understand it now.

Once below the stream, what pleasure
What shall be seen
Awash

I came back to the same shore
Wrapt in mist
Here I laid up my boat. It was
Centuries ago, the black prow
Still there in the sand
And the ghosts walking to and fro, my friends

Perhaps

However that may be there is no other
I would find myself beside
The light over these arenas is dead

It was a nice dream
But I do not know its meaning entirely
No truth that is understood is entire
For wondering I go
Into the crypt where St Martha
Obscured herself from me
Won't you lie under the apple tree
With Our Lady of the Pommiers?
No news is best news from those quarters
And yet silence
Cannot tell all there is to tell nor
Knowledge
Be without silence.

Sillans-la-Cascade

Water falling over these rocks
Like tears
Not for myself, but for another.
Lovely hair, cascading over a brow
Troubled now. I saw her in sleep
So touching and so betrayed.
There is no enemy but the hater.
Once passed, once gone
There is no meeting but in Acheron
Where the full-fledged ghosts wait underneath
And the rock falls
Sisyphus.

What mind from under the dragon's tooth
Sprang in these places, tightened
Between rocks, fastening with chains
The innocent contender, the wise owl
Hoots from the barn.
It is morning under a steel sky,
The horses running;
A splinter of bones and a crucifixion
Against the sky.

Do not ask why I came to this place
To find
What I am better without,
Old memories, sudden as images
On the castle wall,
Armour and hard words.

This is the hour when my bones too
Are ground to powder;
The marrow snivels on to the path
And I am nowhere,
In the pool
Where the cascade falls and Acheron
Opens its gates.
I saw nothing of that in my book
But the mind
Returns to it and it does not leave me.

Entrecasteaux

Entrecasteaux has hatreds
As other cities have loves
So had I but the teeth of the Sibyl

The juniper is bitter and the holm-oak is persistent
The juniper is masked and the holm-oak is hooded
Spring comes down the mountain

The juniper is abundant and the pine bobs before it
Atys your tree upon Mother Ida

Entrecasteaux has hatreds
As other cities have loves
So had I but the teeth of the Sibyl

Spring comes down the mountain to the narrow ravine
Twist your waters, avenging river

Entrecasteaux has houses
With rooms for intrigue and murder
But above all for persistent voices.

Seed-time

Pinpoint seed or seedling I cannot tell which
So deep I look past the petalled leaves
Which once swayed for me as all
So deep
There can be no exchanges or crossed winds
Recognition is one-sided, I am invisible
Or should be, husk of myself.

So a bonfire burns and one looks into it
Fallen ash, green houses
Sticks
Charred till they whiten and the winking lights
Move round the bole.

There could be no meeting again on this earth
In any furrow or perhaps anywhere
Seed-time is a tear-drop carrying the eye
Into the interior of the womb, where hope lies
Crouched for its disappointment.

The Garden

Am I not fortunate in my garden?
When I awake in it the trees bow
Sensibly. There is a church tower in the distance,
There are two, underneath the maze of leaves

And at my back bells, over the stone wall
Fall tumbling on my head. Fortunate men
Love home, are not often abroad, sleep
Rather than wake and when they wake, rejoice.

The Corridor

I

Nothing is what I have done
Where I have been
These long years

No such thing
As metaphysical
Escape
There is a safe
Kind of body begins
With the toe
Continuing through
The bones of the foot:
Must I go
Through every damned bone,
Filament, ligament?

2

Yes, a figure like a light at the end of a corridor
Justice heard her voice
And with attention
Scored
Marks on the brightness
The inexpugnable wall

It was Atalanta ran down
Either foot equal, the hands
Flying like butterflies

3

It is not where I want to go
But I have no choice
Past the buildings, along the straight road
My thoughts with me, I do not want to take them

I plod on
The internal way is best, I am concentrated.
Down on my head a lead weight

Under my feet
The pavement
Rising so hard that my feet are splayed.
Smiling from the side-walk is inappropriate
My intent is serious
A small liar
Heading for an immutable destiny
In whatever disguises
I change my suit several times as I walk

There are dragons at some of the cross-roads
Hedged by privet
Dusty and dull and the long red-brick avenue
Will they reach me in time?
There is hardly a fear, I am so protected
The collar of my rain-coat turned up
The walls of the street and of my eyes so firmly blinded.

You could be lost before day break, if it will
Where are the snares
With which you were threatened?
Where are the entanglements
To trammel your feet and make the way less easy?
The very simplicity is deceptive
It is achieved by the rejection of voice
Touch, smell, taste

No music or shape, that is the best way
Say some

A morass of feet
Mine moving the least certainly among them
There is no way to go on
Which foot is mine?
I can no longer tell, I go all ways
At least there is mire, I am in it, there are others
Is this a walk or a rout?

Where are they going? How many feet have they got?
Where is the rest of them, baulking giants
Without any theory to account for them?

I have my theory, which is just this
From here I set out to there I go.

4

If I opened my eyes, what should I see
Any of this?
A crucifixion, with the blood dripping upon me

Or hands down
Picking a flower
Or exacerbating a butterfly
Taking the wings off a beetle?

Glory to God, three figures
Graces perhaps

5

There is no news Homer among the
Rushes, useless to pry, looking
Here and there in case anywhere there should be

Satyrs, leprechauns there is no news
Homer there is no news. I once saw
Homer advancing and peeping into a dustbin

6

I wanted a way out
From this
Neither can I think
Of any
Except

The paradigm
Of the extended body
Lying in furze
Under the sedge
Or twisted
Under effete grasses, dead also

Surely it stirs
Its moment has not yet come

Yet it will
When

Headlong

Out of the earth
Rising like a jaguar springing

Yet it is not like that
Smooth
Foiled

7

What night
Are you bound for?
Is there any?

I cannot answer that question, I am
Not the man who answers

Who are you then?

Not the man who answers
Not? Not
Not for any man
I am not the man who answers any questions.

Do you ask?

I do not ask
I am not the man who asks

Not? Not

I am not the man who asks

Who are you then?
Not the man
Not the man
Not
Not
Not

8

There is a thread I cannot follow it

There is a way
There is no other
Through darkness

Walk then
Long
Through the corridor

That is not a light then, though it is supposed to be
A lake rather
A guttering candle lights up the surface of it

Black light

I have gone through the door

9

I understand oceans, which do not change
In volume and composition, or not very much
Yet the surface changes, following the day's weather
The depth marches up, the superficial element
Bobs underneath more or less

Movement of sea, volume of water
Moving up from the depths, while the surfaces
Fall, losing themselves
Fathoms
Below, but do not sleep there, turning silently
While the great fish swim through them
– There is no seaweed
Below a certain depth, but –
In palaces
Darkness
The outcome of which
Cannot be guessed.
If there were an encounter
Could it be otherwise than of shadows?

10

The darkening shades are the way I go
How could it be otherwise? I come from lugubrious waters
The hunt and prayer of our hearts

11

Dreams are of no value
They move intangibly
Not turning the wheels
Not moving the limbs
Causing no embrace

12

I walk splendidly, and indirectly
Looking where I am not going
Blowing against closed doors, looking into the open ones.
Monsieur est distrait? He is plain distracted
Old hat askew, travelling boots
Travelling nowhere, or the toes pointed
In the direction opposite to movement, or 30°
Or 37°, or 2.5° or some odd
Measure of distraction from reality.
Behind his spectacles the eyes
Entertain improbable speculations
Rolling, rolling
With little half-movements, aspersions
On this or that aspect of reality.
Why will your feet not take the floor
Those large hands
Close over something not the edge of a mirror?
Dreams are of little value
Old hat, perforated head,
Stuffed with dreams
If that were all

But the direction of movement, the skid and skad
Drawing a circle where there should be a square.
The way it is worth going
Is not an easy one, for intellectual persons
Such as I, nauseous perhaps
To the more intelligent.

Out from under the body politic
Walking in twilight, one after another
Yet a conversation
Hurts, it is a string tied round the body

13

Hanging on a tree in the Garden of Eden
Thirteen days and thirteen nights
Give me some drink: hand me a loaf of bread
Down from the tree, I come and get it myself

There are saws and maxims enough

Before I can sing
Anything that I will
There must first be the elision
Of the individual mind,
Closed like a crack of the earth
The earth itself
Is what I now sing, wish to

14

The backward road
Must be under the marshes
Glutinous, harsh
Darker than ever, resistant
Darker than ever, I would go that way but I cannot

It must be darkness, whether forward or backwards
The light has left me
There is not even a marsh taper, a flicker
A deception one moment believed, though the next doubted
There is not even the taste of death if I go forward
For death is endless
Tasteless, it is infinite
The great cloak
Waiting to be put on
And when I walk in it
I should struggle like a caught thing wanting to use the flesh
Convinced for all eternity that I have it
Torn and feathered like a spent bird
Neither believing
Against my unbelief, nor holding solidly
While these tatters, my flesh
Blow away like salt to the edges of the universe
Death is the only costume I put on
It does not disguise me now, it is my own
Sleep I hoped for
Pre-monitor of the resurrection, mother of language
Leaves me now
Yet there is nothing it leaves
Sleep is for flesh
Such as I used to imagine
Not stretched like mine to the edge of the universe
Compacted marvels
There could be speech with, which, where I now am, is not.
It is not silence, which I have also known, for that is the
    cessation
Of rustling. Where I am now
There are no leaves to stir or cease from stirring

Avert my eyes, I am no longer required
Where the dragons walk, there is certainty
Where the angels
Fling up their trumpets, there is mediocrity
Where peace is
There I would go forward, and not be I
The Incarnation
Came suddenly
In another place, and I no longer stand there

I am on the edge, beyond the touch of reason
As of the flesh
If a word takes me, it is in its flight
From another mouth
It cannot be my ear
Hears

15

The indisputable master of all this,
Old age
Assays no more the gold under his hand
The ways you did not follow matter more
Than those you did
That is why eyes look past
The things you love to those you did not love
The hand is cupped
To catch the silence as it falls between
The chatter that you did not want to hear:
The man who would be off is dead already.

The Noyade

*This is not a satire, nor indeed an invention of any kind. The Fifth
Edition of the* Dictionnaire de l'Académie Française, *published in 1813,
has a supplement containing the new words which had come into use since
the Revolution, with new senses for some old words.*

The vocabulary of the Revolution, it seems,
Was much the same as the one we use at present,
   Which shows that in liberating the human spirit
   The *grands ancêtres* provided amusement for centuries.

Administration centrale is one of these,
As also the *administrations intermédiaires*
   With the *administrateurs* and the *adjoints*
   Engaged in the new administrative employments.

A also contains the useful word *amendement*
In the sense of a 'modification proposed to a draft
   Of a law or decree to render it more precise';
   Why else should anyone propose an amendment?

There is also *anglomane* and *anglomanie*,
Which sounds odd now, but England was then the exemplar
   Of an imagined liberty which attracted the writers
   Who, then as now, wrote faster than they understood.

Aristocrate – it was nothing to do with aristocracy;
But 'the name given to the partisans of the old régime'
   – A kind of lying which has been improved on since:
   Think a moment and you will remember our words.

In A I might also mention *arrestation*,
'The act of arresting a person', much practised by citizens
   Who regarded the appellation 'subject' as odious
   And declined to pronounce it, in their political chatter.

B was for *barrières* 'placed upon the frontiers,
With offices designed for the collection of taxes'
　　Though one knows that, in fact, the barriers had other uses:
　　There was no more going abroad without a passport.

Bureau central, bureaucratie, bureaucratique
Place, function and qualification are now universal;
　　It was, after all, for mankind in its generality
　　That the Revolution was made, not for those who inhabited

A mere particular village, town, city or country.
C: and observe the history of *carmagnole*,
　　'The name at first of a dance, and then a shirt,
　　Afterwards of the soldiers who wore that uniform':

Finally – because a soldier is only a soldier
When he is used by somebody, *carmagnole* achieved a new
　　dignity
　　As 'the designation of a certain kind of report
　　Treasured in the bosom of the National Assembly'.

I say nothing of *centimètre* and *centralisation*,
Citoyen, civisme – 'the zeal which inspires the citizen' –
　　Or *carte de sûreté* – something for paid-up members –
　　Or *club, conscrit*, or *conscription militaire*.

O Liberation! those were inventive days.
Contre-révolution – but better have nothing to do with it.
　　Démocrate, démocratie – 'is employed at present
　　In the sense of attachment to the popular cause'.

Département, for an administrative area
Bearing no relation to the place people live in;
　　Déporter, 'a revival of the old Roman banishment'
　　You were lucky if you got out: *détention*, imprisonment.

I pass over E – though it covers new kinds of *écoles* –
To arrive at F, and the *fonctionnaire public*;
    Fournée, once the word for a batch of loaves,
    Becomes a cartload of people condemned to the guillotine.

G is for *garnisaire*, 'a man put in garrison
With taxpayers who have got behind with their taxes';
    Grand-juge-militaire, 'in each arrondissement';
    Also for *guillotine*, 'perfected by a doctor

To cut off heads by a mechanical operation'.
Homme de loi – H – is the name given to the *légiste*
    'Instructed in the most modern jurisprudence'.
    Indemnité, 'the pay of members of parliament'.

I pass over K, for *kilolitres* of blood,
To get to L, for hanging on lamp-posts or *lanternes*
– Which explains how *liberté* acquired its new meaning
    Of 'doing whatever does no harm to others'.

M, the *majorité*, still of major importance;
Maison d'arrêt, a place of arrest or *détention*;
    Masse, 'collectively, all together, especially
    To go *en masse*, with the crowd, as in an assembly'.

Neutralisation – of treaties, so 'only provisional'
– Unlike the fate of those who suffered in *noyades*,
    Which is pushing a boatload of unpopular people
    To the middle of a river, after making suitable plug-holes.

O, *organiser*, in the sense of 'organising
All the interior movements of any body';
    Passer à l'ordre du jour, as in an assembly,
    To avoid the discussion of anything too awkward.

P is the *Panthéon français*, designed for the cinders
Of those who are favourable to the Revolution;
   Permanence, in the sense that a public assembly
   May be *en permanence*, and never stop talking.

Préhension, for the seizing of any commodity
Which has been made the subject of price regulation;
   And *propagande, propagandiste*, a body or person
   Charged to promote the most acceptable principles.

Q – a *Quiétiste*, used to designate persons
Who do not join in the fun of the Revolution;
   And a *question préalable* is simply the Question
   Of whether a Question had better not be discussed.

For R we have *radiation*, the rubbing out
Of the names of people you are advised to think no more of;
   Réfractaire, for those who have proved refractory
   And therefore must be excluded from their functions.

Réquisition, 'not only used of commodities
But of young men who are needed for military service'.
   S for *septembrisade*, a general massacre,
   And the verb *septembriser* – 'she was septembred'.

Souverain – 'the universal collection of citizens'
– Except the *suspects*, suspected of being indifferent;
   Which brings us to T and to Terror,
   Terroriste, terrorisme, in the end thought slightly excessive.

Travailler is working, but not in the sense of producing
Anything more substantial than disaffection
   'In favour of a faction'; and T is also *tyrannicide*
   – Only be careful that you name the right tyrant.

The alphabet is exhausted with U and V;
Urgence, 'the pressing need for a resolution',
    – A *résolution urgente*, there are no others.
    V, *vandalisme*, 'destroying the arts and sciences'.

V has a final fling with *vociération*,
'A clamorous way of proceeding in assemblies';
    And *visites domiciliaires* – you can guess who visits.
    The man they are looking for might have written this.

Swimming the Horses

To Pippa and David

Swimming the horses at Appleby in Westmorland
– Or Cumbria as they now call it, God damn their eyes.
The rest of the verses *desunt*: they were meant to say
Damn all politicians and bureaucrats
Who cannot make fires with uncertain materials.
They imagine that their voices will be heard above
The ripple of rivers and the song of cuckoos –
Which they will not be, or not for long
If they continue with their inordinate charges
To feed reputatious mouths, or none at all
And think that generations of mud-eaters
Can be stamped out to serve a committee slicker
– As they can indeed, but eaten by a dust
That will soon settle over the whole of England.
Those who kick their ancestors in the teeth
Prosper for a time, but in adversity,
Which soon comes, there is a change.

The Weather

The weather is most noticeable, for what else
Should I notice, I who have become wrapped
In my own silence, no word saying anything
Although I speak it? Others' words come gently,
Like breezes, they are of uncertain origin
They come round a bush with surprise, through the willows,
A heron carries them. If there were any speech
It would be of roses, blackberries trailing
Over the effete comfrey. Spoiled is the world
Spoiled, autumn says, and so say I.
Neat words then, better than none at all,
Talking of nothing while night falls.

Ulysses

Ulysses in your boat
In the curved waters where the eddies are
As the stream turns

                    an old dressing-gown
Swirling in the water
                    round and round
Where is Sackcloth?
                    drowned drowned drowned.
Out from the river-mouth
                    into the sea
Ulysses, traveller, glides on top

Out on the incalculable sea, new stories
Ringing in his ears, he has made them up,
Towards the Pillars
Standing at the edge of the desolate sea
Or so they think
Edges beyond edges

What fell
Over the bridge, into the river, is here before them
A ghost
Laughing in the mists beyond the Pillars of Hercules
(I have no desire to continue this)
Beyond the Pillars

I want to know which way they went
Which way they were delivered
One pole toppled over, the sky
Full of stars, showering the boat fore.
Aft, like a wake, the bubbles receded
That sky dying out

Having departed from Circe
In a small boat with a few educated companions
Who understood that subtraction
And did not want mercy, they were too advanced for it

Peace now, under the wind
Under the keel the barnacle
Considers

Baffled like a ghost tied to the mast, unwillingly
I went from Circe
Torn by the wind, fastened by recollection
Over the peak
Of one wave falling into the trough of another
I had come over vast times as well as waters
Africa on one side, Spain on the other
I do not remember when I drifted through
Into the Atlantic drain

It does not matter how the dice fall, here on shipboard
She runs south homing on the mountain of purgatory.
It is the whirlpool. The wind came from the mountain
Like a whiplash. The boat gurgled and fell

A curl of smoke
Rose from the conical mountain against a blue
Paler than light.

Troia

So in the morning light she came to him
Light-footed

But Troy the common grave of Europe and Asia
Troia (nefas)

The Sibyl's cave
Aeneas standing there
and it was only a descent

ad inferos
Speaking any words
wildly
Hair streaming: Aeneas founding a city
among the dead
Troy speaking again
only through the mouths of the dead
the city pardoned
the libation poured out and the ox-hides spread

I noticed this peculiarity in Troy
That the soldiers, looking out over the walls
Were sightless, they had long been dead
and a Roman capital
Stood in the desert, half broken.

The Desert

1

This is the only place that I inhabit:
The desert.
No drop of water: no palm trees: nothing.
No gourd, no cactus: sand
Heaped on all sides like mountainous seas
To drown in.
Luckily I cannot see myself, I am alone
No mirror, glass, plastic left by an Arab
Nothing
I cannot say it too often
Nothing.
The sand itself would diminish if I said yes.
No rascally Bedouin,
Praying mantis, or nice people
– A mirage of them, occasionally.
But they are not there, any more than I,
For all my vocables, eyes, 'I's,
Other impedimenta of the desert
– Khaki shirt, shorts, chapli,
Mess-tin, for nothing to eat;
Water-bottle, nothing in it.
It is an amusing end, because desired.

2

Alone
But to say 'alone' would be to give validity
To a set of perceptions which are nothing at all
– A set as these words are
Set down
Meaninglessly on paper, by nobody.
There were friends, they have faded into the distance;
With my disintegration the vision becomes blurred,
Rather, disintegrated, each bit

For all I know
Tied to a separate nothing, not I.
Enough of laughter, which echoes like a tin eccentric
Round the edge of the desert:
Tears would be ridiculous
If I could shed them,
Eyes shed them, one
Then another again, weeping
For different things, not joined.

Shatter the retina so that the eyes are many
– Hailstones, now, it can be sand for all I care.
The damned unrepairable, I sit
Like a vehicle sanded up, the desert
Is frequent with images.
Could night come, that would effect a change,
But the sun blazes:
'I am all you have to fear, extreme, hot, searing
But the end is dust, and soon.'

The Zodiac

And so we need divide the year;
Also, the human character.
Aries at first, Aries the Ram
Whose neighbour in the sphere I am:
Taurus who, lowing for Europa,
Must be content with grass for supper;
The other neighbour being Gemini,
Though two might be thought two too many.
Cancer crabs everyone in sight
And therefore has the shortest night,
While Leo tries to be benign
In spite of his ferocious sign.
Virgo, we all know, cannot last
Even until the summer's past;
Her Libra seeks to equalise
With equal balances of lies,
Though Scorpio would bite the tail
Of any too ambitious male
And Sagittarius shoots arrows
At aeroplanes, and brings down sparrows.
Capricorn is a goat, and cannot
Conduct himself as if he were not;
Aquarius with watery eye
Does nothing else but cry, cry, cry;
Pisces, however, swims in tears
Till harmless Aries re-appears.

Why quarter and divide in three?
Too much brilliant astronomy:
The heavens would not stay still, and grew
Quickly to circle out of true,
Till all the scholars, from their book,
Knew that the sky must be mistook.
Then came a learned supposition
That the erroneous position

Taken by the wandering stars
Must reflect on the characters,
Not of astronomers and pedants
But all the new-born innocents
Who had not yet twisted their minds
Into the pattern of mankind.
In case the constellations faltered,
Science would see that they were altered:
So anything you care to hope
Is enlarged in your horoscope;
Whatever makes you shake with terror
Is grimmer in the written error.

If Aries only were a ram
And Gemini, twins in a pram,
Taurus among the cows, and Cancer
Not so much favoured as the lobster;
If Leo kept his woolly head
Inside his cage, and Virgo's bed
Were no more visited than most;
If Libra weighed up pounds of tea
And Scorpio died of DDT,
Who'd be afraid of Sagittarius
Or find no life-belt in Aquarius?
If Capricorn were only goat,
The fear of butts would be remote,
And indeed, but for scholarship,
Pisces might end as fish and chips.

A Baby Asleep in a Passing Car

Sleep your way into the world,
Baby pressed against the glass.
The car moves on, nothing that passes
Does not enter your dream;
Sorrows and mechanical penetrations
Will not escape you. Your mind
Opens like a rose on smiles,
But is nothing, it must wither, change, fall
Before the ripened hip holds – too compactly –
The little you could learn.

The Garden of the Hesperides

If I knew what to say, I would say it;
But as I do not, I send it,
This:
When there was time and place, I lost it;
Now there is not, I regret it:
That.

⋆   ⋆

Faithful, ingenious, I mean to say, witty,
She-Jesuit, you are the writing on the wall

Or I am the wall and you are the writing;
Would I understand, if I knew my letters?

Will you teach me? What if I am ignorant?
Beyond teaching, savage? A kind of faithfulness

I read, although there is none, of the understanding,
In which the writing has erased the wall.

Or suppose you are the wall and I am the writing;
On your witty surface the lines are erased.

What did they say? Mene, Tekel, Upharsin,
Three names for doom. There is one word for pleasure.

⋆   ⋆   ⋆

O, 'I' and 'you' are two conceptions
Neither of which is justified;
Neither 'you' by 'I', nor it cannot be,
'I' by 'you' exactly.

One could imagine talking;
We know better than that.
What is said is what is what,
And that is in doubt.

We could imagine looking
At a world not there;
Eating perhaps or drinking
In the thin air.

Conversation is not
Where there is not I.
Who spoke? Who draws breath?
Not I.

           *   *   *   *

However, something has happened. The thin air
Is certainly thinner and finer than before:
I can see things. It is not that there is light
Anywhere in particular, unless it is every night
Has its moon, every day its sun,
Equal everywhere. Trees tower and streams run
Everywhere lights. Animals come out
In broad daylight fearless, minnow and trout
Agitate in a water clear as air.
What is the meaning of this? The meaning is where
The objects are, it does not bother me.
All of us are disproven, but gently.

           *   *   *   *   *

Not yet said, because unsayable,
Not yet read, and unsayable,
Star enclosed in a vocable.

Absurdity, when to be absurd
Is more than the fortune of being heard.
What is there that is less than a word?

           *   *   *   *   *   *

My object is to say, there may be you,
Equal in nothingness, as in all else:
Therefore the water shines, therefore the dew
Hangs on the grass as big as melons.
What mind is in all this? Not less a mind
Than any pulp within whatever rind.

Apples and oranges is what we are,
And you especially, though side by side
We hung, across the glade seemed far
To me, which was because of pride,
A defect in the garden of the Hesperides
Where all the apples have to do is please.

  *   *   *   *   *   *

You is transferable, the angels say
To you and you and you, a fragrant light
Falling past every soul by day and night.
Whether this may be so, I know no way
Of proving, beyond the happiness of today.

For Passing the Time

For passing the time it is a very good thing
To say, Oh, how are the vegetables growing?
How are the artichokes? Are the leeks coming on?
Will there be decent parsnips when the time comes?

I expect so: nature does not deny her abundance
To those who are patient and don't expect too much;
The leaves wither, and the leaves sprout again;
It is unchangeable as change can be.

Down by the river there are events
In every season; and the river flows
In all seasons, sometimes more, sometimes less:
It is hallowed time which passes along its banks.

But for me how can the time be hallowed?
I seek no remedy in it; there can be none.
The scent of rosemary is pungent in the nostrils:
Break the lavender stem, and recorded time.

Leaves

Leaves are plentiful on the ground, under the feet,
There cannot be too many, they lie below;
They rot, they blow about before they are rotted.
Were they ever affixed to trees? I do not know.

The great connection is from the leaf to the root,
From branch, from tendril, to the low place
Below the burial ground, below the hope of the foot,
The hand stretched out, or the hidden face.

On all occasions, or most, remember this:
Then turn on yourself like a small whirlwind of leaves.

The Goldfish

Everything that is beautiful must be taken away
As that goldfish was. Shining, and plated with gold,
Its mouth trembling, its eye stony with solitude
– I gasped when I saw it; it was my own cry.

The Resurrection

'He seeks to see it all again
In the resurrection.'
And yet it is not so, the sap
Is missing for the hope, perhaps.
The young man puts his hand around
A virgin waist, and in a bound
Is ten feet tall, and full of hope
In his own, not another's, growth.
A small life will creep out, to give
Him his instruction not to live.
Good-bye to hope when that is born.

The Whale

Think nothing of the whale: you may be sure
He thinks nothing of you, and since the grand cetacean
'Conversing chiefly in the northern seas'
Makes no mention of you in his conversation

Except for an expletive when you come near him
– An expletive which is not hard to explain
In view of the charming way in which you accost him –
Why should you exercise your brains about him?

After all, he has the more sizeable body
And who are you to threaten his majority
By exhibiting more brains than he has himself?
It is against the supremacy of his thoughtlessness.

Jonah went into the belly of the whale
And prayed when he got there. Is it a mark of enlightenment,
Perhaps to swallow the whale and then assert
That empty seas are an improvement on creation?

An Afternoon

After the harsh weather the first day of spring:
Even, on the river, someone in a canoe
– And, in the soil, the worms turning.

The pushing buds look up enquiringly:
'Shall we push?' as they do, like children who enquire
Only to be told nature may have its way.

I am past nature and may not have mine
Which is the way of all flesh, and so peculiarly
That of the generality of men

And so peculiarly not mine, but this
World's which, this February afternoon
Looks at me like a May morning.

The Time of Year

She asks me how I do
It does not matter how
Well and ill are all the same
Now.

I live beyond touching
Beyond friendship now
Do not ask oh do not ask
It does not matter how.

★

The night has gone from me
And the day is going
Oh the world oh the world turns
And I on it.

Who, I? Or the world itself
Turning, turning
Between the moon and the clouds
Its head spinning.

★

What price the cul-de-sac
Where you must certainly go?
Patience is getting in
– And the rest you know.

Know it as unknowing
No-way-to-go, unknown.
The fields whisper to harvest
– You go home.

★

A Stray

Oh it is pale, is pale, this afternoon
Like that blue flower, strayed in my garden
Chive or marsh-plant perhaps or some pale bloom
Straggled out of the night

Paleness is light
Defect of darkness, mother-of-pearl, pearl
In a dark ocean heaving all around.

O turn away
Wind, from me

Turn away light
Fail into watery light
And underline the hills
Till they come to night.

The Hedgehog

The garden is mysterious at night
And scented! and scented! in the night of stars.
The hedgehog snuffles somewhere among leaves,
Just by the arch-way. So it is with time
– Mute night and then a voice that says nothing,
Busying itself, complaining and insisting:
When this has end, silence will come again.

The Forest of Dean

in memory of Francis Webb (1913–1975)

The forest is immutable they say:
There by the pond it seems so, for one day
– Great oaks, dark water, that is what I see
And yet the blood dries underneath the tree.
Are you there, Francis? Were you ever there?
A heavy body thinner now than air
As oaks determine in a smaller thing
Than acorns, dust or wind, as fish can bring
Their images to nothing when they sink
And there is no more than a thought to think.
That least of things! A trace that is no more
Than a lost ripple on a watery floor.
So you, now nothing, may be called to mind
But not to conversation with your kind.
In the great kitchen where you last fell down
There was you gasping, but no other sound
– The kitchen clock perhaps, or your wife's cry,
But it was you alone who had to die.
Now one earth covers you and her, in turn
I stood beside your grave-sides, not to mourn
But, *Salve atque vale!* and now here,
Where you were young, there is no place for tears.

The May-Boy

This is a term, picked up locally, for a stray potato – I suppose originally for a child born under a hedge.

Poor scattered bastard, straggling out of the row
And out of kind, green where the earth is brown!
As for tomorrow, beyond meditation,
Under the haulms plump the insistent tubers
Which nature had intended, but not I
– Willing to take over the garden tomorrow
And fruit remorselessly when I die.

Two Capitals

'Sieg Heil! Sieg Heil!' It came then like a roar
Across Berlin in nineteen thirty-four.
Herr Bargel, Dr Mohrhoff and young Schmid
Answered its echo like a natural need.
By the old Reichstag torches lit the sky
As the brown-shirted Fackelzug went by.
The heart of Germany! But not my heart;
I stood with thousands but I stood apart.
What peace for England? That is all I knew,
The awful menace of a dream come true.
And France? Months later, there was I, as one
At table, rue du cardinal Lemoine,
At breakfast, lunch and dinner: René Chave,
Febrile as autumn, nineteen and a half;
Old Monsieur Duchemin, discoursing reason;
Madame, who bought the vegetables in season
And clacked over the price of artichokes;
Jacques who irrupted with his silly jokes;
Hélène who once let slip an awful word;
The Madame Picart who was so refined,
Contrasting English Sport with the French Mind;
Henri her studious son, who chose the latter;
Kreitmann, who had his own thoughts on the matter
As on most others. What do I make of it,
Forty-five years later, in Somerset?

Winter has come and I welcome it
Despite grey cloud which hammers down its lid
Upon the flat world, flat as it, and still.
Oh, it is cold, but not with that cold will
Which laid itself over the multitude
That hurried, clouded, gathered or just stood
Below me in the Schäferkampsallee.
There it was cold, there there was steel to glint
If in no more than in a massive hint

As the leaves fell, had fallen. Yet again
Can I not feel it in the icy rain
Threatening to fall over gabbling Europe?
I am too well instructed to have hope.
Yet softly, do not speak. Only prepare
To walk out naked in the bitter air
Trusting what is not to be trusted, love.

Athelney

The apple trees are dulled in the red sun,
The fruit unpolished and the day is done.
This is where Alfred crept by on his marsh,
Wet straggling country still, but now the harsh
Road runs on blue and dark beside his ghost.
Headlamps begin to count the sodden posts
And catch a nosing heifer here and there.
The squawking ducks are home, and the wet air
Settles more heavily as the night comes.
'A bit of fire-stuff, like': a voice close by
And a dead branch is dragged to Athelney.

The Rose

She looks towards the south
As all such roses do,
So, away from the house
And away from you.

She looks after the rose
Far, and far away
And all is in decline,
Even the day.

Nightshade

Enchanter's nightshade is
Of all flowers the least;
I saw her poisoned sister
Gleam from the hedge.

Wild wood-bine, cover her,
Sloe, move away!
And yet it is she
Remains in memory.

Teazles

Teazles in the swamp
With the convolvulus
Climbing among them, the willows
Backing them up.

So plenty, although it is poor
And in decay!
Harsh world, where all is
And nothing stays!

Thistles to lamb's wool
And the nettles fade:
No need to be here
When spring comes again.

Frost

A single fisherman in the icy water
And the river red with the sun;
He lifts his rod to the bank, winding, and packs
Then clumsily runs

Along the bank, his breath like a kettle's
In the frosty air.
I pass on the hard mud of the drove:
No-one else there.

The fields are winter now, the mallard fly
Thoughtfully, nowhere to land in the hard pools:
So am I thoughtful, less thinking than looking.
Words are for fools.

Therefore I write this, to show that I am with them
With an empty mind
– And a loose tongue, the indispensable appurtenance
Of human kind.

A Purgatory

Old people, hammering
Across the table
Their mutual disagreements
As they are able.

One says: 'Lay them out there,
The bulbs.' The other
Objects – nothing else to object to
And there must be bother.

Seventy creeps on to eighty;
Half-blind eyes
Round the kitchen table, shielded from the north wind
And the open skies.

Stepping heavenward over the rubble
Of enough years, battles, importance;
The meaning has gone, the quarrel remains
Till the last cornice.

In the West Country

The rooks rise, the pee-wits rise
Mud on the ground, cloud in the skies
Enough space for all those wings
Caw said it, the pee-wits signalled
Pouring over the empty skies.

I am alone within the circle
Of low hills, I know its ways
Somerton Moor, slight hills, great girdle
Green floor and most open days
None walks here without intention
Even I, when here, have mine
But the floors of all the oceans
Have no depths more submarine
Here we are under the heavens
As under waters, birds are fish
The sky changes, a shadow passes
As it were a passing ship.
No place for anything, the extreme
End of the world, whether depths or shore
A finger of sea merely a lane
Whether from after or to before
Time falters but March will come
And break the pee-wits into pairs
With slow flight and mournful cries
And spring the sun-shine in the air.

So it is with Engellond.
Whose bones rest here? Who was found
Lying there beside King Arthur?
Whose bones followed after
Everywhere through the land?
Not a thing one can understand
Name nor yet enumerate.
Yet we are with it and the great

Ancestors lie with the small
Not disturbing us at all
Yet we inhabit with them all
And cannot forget them, or if we do
It is not because they ask us to:
Even Brutus who came from Troy
And landed at Totnes, so they say,
Fought with giants, like that of Cerne
Who held the island in those times.
So it was. That much is firm.
Whether the whole British race
Sprang from him, may be doubted.
But at Ozleworth I dare say lie
Some of them and you will find
My ancestors among the rest.
Elias Wyrloc not least
For he lived before Polydore
Somewhere there on the Severn shore
Though he was an outrageous Saxon
– The best stock, when all's said and done.
How do I trace myself from that?
It does not matter, it can't be done.
Yet that man who climbs Rat Hill
Is my brother, I know him still:
And that woman is half my mother
Who passed Pig Hill with a basket of eggs
Three hundred years ago, if you will
Or four hundred, it does not matter.
All gone now? It is perhaps
And nothing can make it more than that.
Who was it, from Ilminster
Spire, as he calls it – it is a tower –
Found the English people missing?
But they are there about their business
As in other places, Birmingham
Say or Hull or Immingham
– I mention such unlikely places

For I have seen as many faces
Of my compatriots, perhaps more:
More, certainly, rich and poor.
A soldier who had lost a thumb
And came to visit where the trams
Screeched to a halt, 1918;
A queue outside the chapel hall
Waiting not for jobs but the dole;
A thumb without a soldier, found
Later, upon Irish ground.

By Mina Road I crossed the Frome
Hic, illic, I knew it had come
Past beeches near Oldbury Court.
The Fleet runs underground, the Lea
Has no swans now. I know what ought
To be, what is and that they are
The same. I love the squalor
Of the long cut which used the air
From Warwick Road to the Horsefair,
I walked along it to save the fare.
I am at home in Stapleton Road.
You cannot frighten me with cities
Or exact a fallacious pity
From me, for I know them all,
The posh people, the smaller, the small.
I know the gentle boy whose mother
Was gaoled for stealing from the workhouse.
There were bare feet in Freeland Buildings
And Berkeley Street. And I knew Pooch,
Beaten, precarious,
Son of a drunk in the old style.
The well-to-do had only a smile
A plant in the front room, and fear
Of less before the end of the year.
These horrors are not horrors to me
But only a picture of what must be.

What was has this advantage
That it is truer than what is
For that is gone in a moment
And the future never comes.
Irremediably old, as old is
I could do worse than look at water
The floods shining between the willows.
Unnoticeable time has gone
The inconsiderate hours have run:
I stand like time still.
Nothing but folly in the will
And amor vincit omnia.
Myself whom time devours
Heard love once, louder than any
What seemed an end was a beginning,
Now ending, as life does. All
That has passed this way is magical
No wonder therefore if the light
Falls upon England tonight
Extenuating what is ill.
Others may hope but not I
Yet what may be tried
Crossing the stream
To drop a pebble in.

Sleep

The nights are horrible: I lie awake
Caged in a body that is in decay
As are all human things. Night, you are empty
And I am full of ingratitude.

Sometimes I rise and watch the great moon
Inquisitively at the study window:
The clouds fly over it with a laugh;
Perhaps the moon herself is sardonic.

And yet sometimes she has a troubled face
But if I pity her I pity me;
Neither is in need of such attention:
I have only to wait for the last day.

But what comes indeed is day at last,
A new morning, ordinary like the others,
Nothing intimidating, the smallest hopes
Serve to plaster over the wound of night.

And yet enough remains for me to say:
Sleep is my home, sleep is where I belong.
It is not night but this exultation
Awaits me at the last but, oh, how long?

Anglicans

She was down on her knees before the grate
In the cold rectory, crossing a few sticks
To make a little flame look like a fire.
How long her fingers, long and slim her arms!

Then suddenly she sat back on her hams
And gazed, interrogating, serious,
Up at the heavy marble mantelpiece
Yet had no question for it, I felt sure.

But all her straight back and her jutting face,
With so fine nose and chin, and so fine lips
Must have been asking something – not of me
Who sat there as a stranger in the house.

How had her thirty summers for they were
Still summers with a touch of early spring
Come to this house to be obedient
To all the rector's nearly seventy winters?

He stood there now above her, slight and grey,
With bones as fine as glass and silver hair,
A scholar in direct line, as it seemed
From himself more than fifty years before.

Father and daughter they might well have been,
But they were man and wife, and still surprised
To find themselves alone with one another,
Still waiting for a third to turn the page.

All this was long ago, and I imagine
The girl herself septuagenarian
Hardly recovered from her first surprise
Doing the church flowers with her long hands

And knowing no-one in the congregation
Of the too-bustling village she had found
Far from the parish where she left her rector
To turn to dust in the appointed ground.

The Broken Willow

It was an old willow with a dark
Hawthorn bush underneath its leaning stem.
(The bush was dark not because of shadow
But from the rustling silver of the willow

Poring over it like an attentive head.)
Over the stile and to the river-side
I went to examine this conjunction.
It was no girl poring over a lover

Or comforting a child dark but her own.
It was an old broken sexless thing
Which time had ripped open and its tubes
Rings and soft places open in their rot,

Yet more like a circuit than a man,
A control panel with the cover off,
Saving a natural grace, a contentment
Of ruin sinking into renewed life.

Vigil and Ode for St George's Day

Déjà il ne cherchait plus le bonheur
RENÉ BÉHAINE

What is the cure for the disease
Of consciousness? The cures are three,
Sex, sleep and death – two temporary
And only one that's sure to please.

In sex the circles of the mind
Close to a point and disappear
And that is something, till we hear
The world again and are not blind.

Sleep closes round us from without
Until it has us in its grip
And then the pincers start to nip:
It tells us what to dream about.

And death? Then all is gone, or so
There is best reason to believe.
In manus tuas: what we leave
Is certain, and enough to know.

For we are stone, or so they say
And how should we have ears to hear
Any objection, we who are
The treaders of the obvious way?

Either the truth is what we see
Or else it is not to be seen.
No more is it, perhaps; that green
Is grass, that tall thing is a tree.

But what else is it cunning men
Invite the suckers to believe?
All manner of follies weave
Their ways past us with if and when.

Yet there is truth which we assert
And I myself would die for one
If there were need, as there is none:
Better the world should be inert.

There is a time, it is enough
To know, there have been, will be times
And places when and where the crimes
Habitual to mankind, grow rough.

But we can rest in comfort, no
Mind need assert what all betray.
We in the light of common day
Without concern watch the light go.

So must it be, that only death
Relieves us at the sentry-box;
The guard comes marching up, the flocks
Of augurs' birds catch at our breath.

I watched them once, when harmlessly
They flew as martins near the house,
Dipping and soaring, and could rouse
No trouble but in memory.

A line of sceptical recruits,
Myself among them, waited for
What fortunes there might be in war
But no-one found the one that suits

Because no fate is suitable
To any man who hopes for more
Than comes his way, or comes before
He has decided it is well.

For fortune like the birds that fly
Takes its direction from the wind
Which no man changes or holds pinned
And which blows on us till we die.

The first, the bitter lot of all,
Is to be born, for so it is
As time and place and parents please
Or rather, as their fortunes fall.

Then come the choices: none is right
For none is as the birds allow;
By Aldebaran and the Plough
They pass, we into darker night.

That much is tolerable, but that
The same should swallow up our land
May not be borne, and yet the hand
Points to the hour that we are at.

The time that bore us runs away,
The place must follow, the extreme
Edge of the world is here, the dream
Breaks on another homely day.

The strong will always be unjust,
The weak will cringe and run away
Or find their comfort in a day
When they will do as all men must:

And who would dare to boast of that?
We who survive, though not for long,
May envy those who do most wrong
Yet soon enough they too fall flat.

And who is he who in the end
Loves life more than he longs for death?
Does not the most exulting breath
Turn at last to the only friend?

The spirit which was proud to be
Collected in a little earth
Finds what the privilege is worth
And in that knowledge he is free.

Fortune which holds us in its grip
Does not change, though it seems to do,
The same for me, the same for you
Whatever words are on your lips.

For what we say and what we are
Are different things, and we console
Our patience when we take a role:
Only one voice will carry far.

Christ comes to all, because belief
Is necessary for our peace,
The world cannot give it, release
Can only come by way of grief.

The Man of Sorrows is the one
Who represents the way we go:
He is the only one we know
However furious our fun.

For he knows better than the most
Experienced practitioner
Whatever comes to him and her
And that their pleasure is a Ghost.

And of death too he understands
The comfort and the mystery;
The secrets of mythology
Lie always open in his hands.

The bark of Charon and the bite
Of Cerberus, are jokes to him
Yet in his mind no single whim
The pagans have, is lost from sight

For all is laid upon the cross,
The auguries, the sacrifice,
The marching armies, every vice
And virtue, every gain and loss.

There, all was nothing to the God
Who was inside the man, who was
The man and all was all because
He died where Adam first had trod.

The intervening years were gone:
All this he did for Adam's sake
And so the future reeled to take
Another face from that time on.

The face is sorrow, like the Man,
The underworld no longer waits
To have our shadows and our fates
And where our God hung, others can.

He has gone climbing out of space
And time, yet taken with him all
That we have here, the world is small
Beside his new appointed place

Which also leaves him where he was
Before he came, but with a new
Body which he already knew
From his intent to visit us.

Our bodies too, so lifted up,
Will shine as his does, so they say,
But that is for another day
When we have also drunk the cup

Which will not pass, and when we leave
The world we credit now for one
Invisible under our sun
And in which none of us can believe.

So glory, laud and honour, all
To the impossible, and most
To Father, Son and Holy Ghost
And let our own pretensions fall.

They may, but only if we love
No other as we love our end.
The night comes down upon our friends
As on ourselves, yet still above

Their graves, the grass grows and the sun
Shines upon others as on us:
The fieldmouse and the weasel pass
And do not ask whose will is done.

But we, who saw our friends depart
Into the shadows of the moon
Leave others, as it may be soon,
Glad we are gone or, in their hearts

Holding our tiny memory
A moment till that too goes out.
Why not? For we can never doubt
The comfort of mortality.

Yet may Time's treasure still remain
Until it quietly ebbs away
Beyond our knowledge, England's day
– I cannot help it, for the pain

Of her demise is more than all
The mind can suffer for the death
Of any creature that draws breath,
And should her time come round again

Our dust will stir, not to a drum
Or any folly men devise
But to the peace which once our eyes
Met in her fields, or else in some

Of her best children, from the first.
All this is folly too and yet
Rather than any should forget
Let this sad island be immersed

In raging storm and boiling seas.
Let no man speak for her unless
He speaks too for her gentleness
And it is her he seeks to please.

Waking

May has her beauties like another month,
Even June has her pleasures. I lie here,
The insistent thrush does not trouble me
Nor the slight breeze: a tree stump looks like a cat.
Yet all is not altogether well
Because of memory.; crowd round me here
Rather, you ghosts who are to drink of Lethe.
Who else would go back to the upper world
Or take again the nerve-strings of the body
Or will to suffer grief and fear again?
Once I did: and the echo still comes back,
Not from the past only – which I could bear –
But from the young who set out hopefully
To find a bitter end where they began
And evil with the face of charity.
I have seen some such and do not want
Ever to pass along that road again
Where blind beggars hold out their hands for coin
And saints spit in their palms. This I have seen
And shall see if I wake from sleeping now.

Another Waking

Was it a cat squealed or was it metal,
This grincement I heard as I awoke?
A cloud in the sky and a cat under the bed,
Both perhaps startled by my waking.
The cloud steamed forward, lumen de lumine,
A puff of white travelling over the blue.
The cat? There was an impact in the bushes,
I saw it no more than uncertainly.
Incident? Hardly. Machination, dream?
What else is there? Things are what they seem.

The Absence

How can it be that you are gone from me,
Everyone in the world? Yet it is so,
The distance grows and yet I do not move.
Is it I streaming away and, if so, where?
And how do I travel from all equally
Yet not recede from where I stand pat
In the daily house or in the daily garden
Or where I travel on the motor-way?
Good-bye, good-bye all, I call out.
The answer that comes back is always fainter;
In the end those to whom one cannot speak
Cannot be heard, and that is my condition.
Soon there will be only wind and waves,
Trees talking among themselves, a chuchotement,
I there as dust, and if I do not reach
The outer shell of the world, still I may
Enter into the substance of a leaf.

The Hare

I saw a hare jump across a ditch:
It came to the edge, thought, and then went over
Five feet at least over the new-cut rhine
And then away, sideways, as if thrown
– Across the field where Gordon and I walked
Talking of apples, prices and bog-oak,
Denizens of the country, were it not
That denizens do not belong, as they do
And the hare tossing herself here and there.
And I? If I could, I would go back
To where Coombe Farm stood, as Gordon's stands
Trenched in antiquity and looking out
Over immense acres not its own
And none the worse for that. You may say
It is the sick dream of an ageing man
Looking out over a past not his own.
But I say this: it is there I belong,
Or here, where the pasture squelches underfoot
And England stirs, forever to hold my bones.
You may boast of the city, I do not say
That it is not all you say it is
But at the Last Judgment it will stand
Abject before the power of this land.

Thoughts on the Churchyard and the Resting-Places of the Dead

FROM THE GERMAN OF ANDREAS GRYPHIUS

for Kurt Ostberg

I

Where am I now? Is this the ground
In which humility may flower?
Is there refreshment to be found
For those who knew in busier hours
The heat and burden of the day?
And bore the frost of bitter nights
And in the midst of hurts and slights
Took up their share of care and pain?

2

Where am I? Here are the narrow plots
Which hide within their pregnant wombs
What has been sown there by the God
Who can wake corpses from their tombs.
Where some see splendour, I see fear.
Not for me the Hesperides
Or Babylonian luxuries;
I see the best of gardens here.

3

Although here no seductive scent
Streams from the jasmin and the rose,
Although no tulips here present
Their brilliant military shows,
Though here no cultivated land
Grows pomegranates or such-like fruit
It bears here what I long for but
What the world does not understand.

4

O School, in which the best instruction
Is given to us mortal men!
No pages full of false deductions
And no delusive apophthegms.
While I have passed in vanity
The wasted treasures of my time
The hours spent here instead define
The straight way to eternity.

5

O School, which utterly appals
Those whom the world regards as clever,
Which those for whom repute is all
Or money all, regard with terror.
O School which terrifies the mind
That knows the lot and has no conscience!
O School which offers no emollients
To cut-throats claiming to be kind.

6

O School, which puts men in a sweat
And makes their hair stand upon end
When they are near the judgment seat
But nearer their lascivious friends.
O School, which makes a man's knees knock
And his limbs tremble, cold as ice,
Because with all money can buy
He knows his mind is closed to God.

7

I go to school with you and long
To fathom where true wisdom lies.
Examine me! There's nothing wrong,
You will find, with my ears or eyes.
What Socrates once taught me, now
Is nothing, and the Stagirite
Has quite collapsed. There is no light
In Greek philosophy I know.

8

Who is there now that will explain
The subject that I want to master?
Set out the principles and main
Conclusions that I should hold fast to?
Or can I here and on my own
Sit down and work the answers out
That will put paid to every doubt
That troubles me? No, not alone.

9

What's happening? Is the ground I stand on
Reeling? And is that roar the trees?
Is the earth tearing its mouth open
So as to let the roots get free?
Do I hear dry bones rattling? Say,
Do I hear clamorous human voices?
Is that the south wind getting boisterous?
Or heavy stones, rolling away?

10

I stand and stare. A bitter cold
Freezes my veins, my heart, my lungs.
From my brow streams of sweat have sprung.
I am glued where the ground still holds.
The whole field has become a grave
And all the coffins are revealed.
What dust, brick, plaster once concealed
Is open now and plain as day.

11

O last but still uncertain house!
The refuge into which we creep
Whenever the clock tells the hour
And the rose pales upon our cheek.
That palace, which the world once gave,
Swearing that it would last for ever,
That same world, once our life is over
Destroys to assail us in the grave.

12

You for example were wrapped up
In tin and you perhaps in copper.
And you perhaps once had a flood
Of liquid lead to line your coffin.
You were rich, no expense was spared;
This one, now that I think of it
Had gold and marble in his pit.
Then how is it I find you bare?

13

Ah, greed and fury have not scrupled
To open up the grave's dark night,
And what I sought in pain and trouble
Lies patent in the deathly light.
Ah, lifeless men, no robber's hand
Would have intruded on your rest
Had you seen proper to entrust
Your bones in plain boards to the sand.

14

For even cedars shrink at last,
The rotten pine-boards go to nothing
And the oak's strength is quickly past,
The grave is her grave, no escaping.
Why do you value the light fir?
The joints will always crack and split.
The narrow box will go to bits
However hard you caulk and hammer.

15

God help me. Coffins open wide,
I see the bodies in them move.
The army of the once alive
Begins to exercise anew.
I find myself surrounded by
A host death has deprived of power,
A spectacle which forces showers
Of burning tears from my blank eyes.

16

O spectacle which makes the world
And what the world most values, stink.
I feel my arrogance desert me,
My courage and my folly sink.
Are these the men who ruled our land,
Defied it, knocked it, held on tight,
Who sharpened daggers, swords and pikes
And held it down with bloody hands?

17

Are these the men who mollified
The Father's heart with sighs and prayers?
Who, though distressed and mortified
Dared face his anger with their cares?
Who bewailed nothing but their faults
Though money and possessions vanished,
Though anguish left the body famished,
The oppressed spirit nipped and gnawed.

18

Are these the men who put aside
All trace of decency and shame,
Who brought from hell into the daylight
Abominations without name?
Who piled up crime on crime, who slit
Throats for fun, poisoning the world
Until the hour when they were hurled
With thunder and lightning into the pit.

19

Are these the men who were not stained
By pleasure in their pleasant youth,
Whose young minds were early inflamed
By passionate desire for truth?
Those who now sing before the Lamb
The joyful song not many know
And walk in garments white as snow
In endless peace before I AM.

20

Are these those who once strutted round
In purple, silk and gold, and these
Those who crept by on humbler ground
In hunger, nakedness, disease?
And these those whom envy so roused
They begrudged others even breath?
Whom no land could contain? In death,
In what packed quarters are they housed?

21

Where are the miracles of grace,
Beauties who captured souls by storm?
Of their delights I see no trace,
Only some ghastly heads, deformed.
Where are those whose store of knowledge
Astounded everyone? Who were
Honoured as great philosophers?
Time has demolished the whole college.

22

Now for the most part all I find
Is bones from which the flesh has slipped,
Skulls with no cover of any kind,
Faces without noses or lips,
Heads missing skin or maybe ears,
The brow and cheeks have gone to nothing
And where the lips should be hanging
Only a tooth or two appears.

23

The bones that once made up the spine
And neck, still somehow hang together
But nothing now keeps them in line,
The ribs stick out and they will never
Again hold heart and lungs close pressed;
The chest's as empty as can be,
The contents eaten, similarly
The double pleasure of the breasts.

24

What use now for the shoulder-blades?
The arms have now lost all their strength.
What served the man in all his trades,
The hand that had the management
Of tools and achieved mastery
Of sea, land, air and dared such feats
Of heroism, is in pieces,
Deprived of all activity.

25

The belly empty, hip and shin
And foot are nothing now but bones,
Hollow, misshapen, yellowy green,
Broken and dry like shards or stones.
In thousand-shaped deformities
Deformity is recognised.
Here every quality's disguised,
Young, old, poor, noble, lovely, wise.

26

And these are they against whom time
Has fully carried out its sentence;
There is no trace of flesh or slime
Mortality could take from them.
Far more repulsive are those here
Who wrestle still with putrefaction,
On whom decay pursues its action,
Those who were with us till last year.

27

The pretty ringlets fall away,
The plaits begin to come apart.
Where the moist flesh still has its say,
About the temples, movement starts.
And the unseeing eyes begin
To be unstable, as the worms
Inside the head hatch out and stir,
Wrinkle the nose and break the skin.

28

The lovely cheeks crumple and shrink,
The chin and tongue and teeth show white.
Upon the coral lips black ink
Spreads blots which put colour to flight.
The forehead splits, the snowy throat
Becomes earth-coloured, as if the sun
Which shone above it, had begun
To melt the frost and the soil showed.

29

What whisper comes out through the wind-pipe?
What is that hissing in the breasts?
It seems to me that I hear vipers
Whistling their music with the rest.
What an intolerable vapour
Rises into the frightened air
Made heavy by the poison there!
So is it by the Avernian lake.

30

So steams the marsh of Camarina,
So smoke the yellow dragons' dens.
The tortures of the Japanese
Do no worse to half-strangled men
Than the plague striking from the mist
Which rises from the popping corpses
Bathed in sweet oils not long before
And incense brought from lands far distant.

31

Filth from the guts breaks through the skin
Where the maggots have bitten through.
I see the guts dissolving in
Pus, blood and water. It makes me spew.
The mildewed flesh that time has left
Is gobbled by a snaky mob
Of bluish worms which do the job
As if they revelled in the mess.

32

What is the use of aloes now?
They cannot keep beauty in shape.
What about myrrh? It has no power
To stop the youthful limbs from ageing.
Is what came out of Palestine
Asphalt or flesh? There is no knowing.
We cannot tell, of all these bones,
Which went with which in former times.

33

What use now is a splendid dress
Embroidered with a golden thread?
And is not all this silk now pointless,
Embellishing the banished dead?
See how the purple loses colour
And all that work becomes unpicked,
How quickly patterns are unfixed
Which once cost hands so much endeavour.

34

You dead! Ah, what I learn from you!
What I am, what I shall become,
A little dust that the wind blew
Is all I carry to the tomb.
How long will my body persist?
How soon shall I conclude my years?
Say good-bye to those left here
And go where time does not exist?

35

Shall I be able to prepare
Thoughtfully for the long journey?
Or shall I have no time to spare
When I am called whence none returns?
Do not be sudden, Lord of Life,
Or send for me without warning!
But be with me on that last morning,
Protector, guide, my Way, my Light.

36

Where shall I leave my lifeless body,
Entrust it to the final grave?
How many, thinking to make ready,
Have their tombs built, but yet in vain!
How many lie in unknown sand?
Who can guess how chance may fall?
How many has the ocean rolled
To throw up in an unknown land?

37

It does not matter very much
Whether I'm married or lie alone,
Lord, so long as I may touch
Your garment, pleading at your throne.
I see the appointed hour like some
Tremendous prelude with great crashes
Of thunder and great lightning flashes,
And soon eternity will come.

38

When, amidst prodigies and trumpets,
We hear God's final battle-cry
Echoing through every land in triumph
Announcing death itself must die,
When marble, copper, metal, stone
And Pharaohs' tombs from their long night
Deliver to the air the light
And re-invigorated bones;

39

When the sea gives up its dead
Casting up thousands on the shore
From its deep gulfs and tangled weed
The bodies that the Judge has sent for,
When what the north wind blew off course,
What tigers ate up in Morocco
Or flames devoured in Persia,
What rivers that were sown with corpses;

40

What the Brazilian cannibals
Ate, wilder than their own wild beasts,
And those whom appetite for gold
Buried beyond hope of release;
When what Vesuvius overwhelmed
With burning ash and blazing sparks,
What Ætna buried beyond help
Or Hekla spat at in the dark;

41

When what time winnows in the air
Will suddenly be whole again;
Prisoners, however deep they are
In dungeons, will become free men
To see the Son of the Most High
Come in glory and put to shame
His foes, and in his Father's name
Sit where all causes will be tried.

42

Now hear how the Judge will pronounce
His principal and final sentence,
He who himself was judged here once
And bore it for me with all patience,
Who gives new light from heaven above:
How he makes earth dissolve, and breaks
The heavens asunder! Here stand and quake
The Jesus-haters, the Jesus-lovers.

43

Those whom I see here now without
Distinguishing one from the other
I shall see (as I cannot doubt)
Plunged into joy or sorrow, either
Into joy more than sense can know
Or sorrow such as none felt before,
Into delight for evermore
Or everlasting loss and sorrow.

44

Joys that the world cannot contain,
Sorrow before which Hell will reel,
Pleasure that destroys all pain,
Sorrows none here could bear to feel,
Pleasures that will drown all cries,
A sorrow that is pure despair,
Bliss which leaves no place for care,
Sorrow so keen it never dies.

45

Then I shall see you in your skins,
Free from corruption, with full veins;
All that before was hidden in
The grave, will be alive again.
I'll see you, but how different!
Transfigured some, O what delight!
Others disfigured, terrifying!
Joy! I shall shout, and then lament.

46

I'll see you shine with more brilliance
Than would be in ten thousand suns.
I'll see you and avert my glance
From those who have no consolation,
See some more beautiful than beauty,
Some uglier than ugliness,
Some finding comfort, some the darkness
Pregnant with ghosts and devilry.

47

Many the world called good and great
God's sentence designates as lost.
Many spat on and reprobate
Are chosen for the heavenly host.
Never mind how the marble reads,
Epitaphs may be pitched too high.
Corpses however cannot lie
Nor this Court ever be deceived.

48

The corpse shows that you must decline
In rottenness and stink to dust,
That nothing in the world's too fine
To go to ashes when it must,
That though we are not equal here
In death there is equality.
Go and prepare your case and be
Wide awake when the Judge appears.

49

He alone knows how to distinguish
In the confusion death has brought
Who will depart to endless anguish,
Who find the peace that they have sought.
He ensures that no single speck
Of dust from bodies shall escape him.
Air, wind and water keep from him
Nothing, in spite of time and death.

50

You dead! Ah, what I learn from you!
What I was, what I then shall be!
What is eternal, what is true!
No more the world shall trouble me.
Oh you who lie there, teach me so
To stand, that when I end my days
And take leave of the world, I may
Leave Death, and find Life where I go.

News

They live in the excitement of the news.
Who is what? What is that? And is the noise
I hear from an important quarter? When
Is what to happen? Who is what, finally?

Finally nobody is anything,
That is the end of it, my busy friend
And just as what you hear has no beginning
It has, assuredly, no certain end.

The end that comes is not the end of what,
The end of who perhaps, and perhaps not;
The rattle and the flashing lights are over,
Death is overt, but all the rest lies hidden.

Think what you will, nothing will come of that,
What you intend is of all things the least;
As you spin on the lathe of circumstance
You are shaped, it is all the shape you have.

Up the Arts!

Shall we make legends of our silly selves?
The lies invented by the semi-great,
By Yeats for example, cut no ice:
After a few years the truth shows through
And where is folly or invention then?
The folly heightened, the invention fallen,
The bright surface cracks, and underneath
The muddy water slinks away to sea
Or lurks still to be lost below the weeds.
All nature will resume her homely sway;
What grew will grow, what was invented, die.

Taxila

There is a rail-head at Havelian
– Or was, for I was there long ago –
Around it a sweet plain circled by hills:
This was my Greece, the only one I know.

It was a ghost of olives that I saw:
I had not seen the Mediterranean light
Where it falls, but I had dreamed of it.
I who had not been born woke to the sight.

Rus in urbe, urbs in the dazzling grey
– Or was it green? – green, but so grey and brown,
A spot of light in the surrounding darkness:
Taxila was the name of the town,

The heart of all I loved and could not have;
And in that limy track, as I approached,
A child with bright eyes offered a coin.
It was a bargain that was proposed.

Would I, the soldier of an alien army,
Neither the first nor last to come that way,
Purchase for rupees certain disused drachmas
Left by the army of an earlier day?

Alexander himself came down from those hills,
Over the mountains beyond them to the north
– Far lands, the boy said, but mine was farther
And longer ago still my setting forth

For my exile burned me like the sun.
I should have bought that coin, I often thought of it
After that time, and in far different places:
It would have carried me over the Styx.

I would have returned, but there is no returning.
Yet you may rise, ghosts, or I sink to you.
The world is in my hand, breathing at last
For now I know, only the past is true.

The Christmas Rose

A spray of myrtle and the Christmas roses
Come from the garden like a grail of light:
They climb out of the mist into a hand
Which holds them till they flower in her sight:

Myrtle for Myrtilus, who died for treachery
And yet found a place among the stars;
The Christmas rose for peace and chastity,
Old stories both, if any of them are.

Yet love remains, although I cannot see it:
The myrtle berries hovering among leaves,
Dark for sorrow, white petals of the rose
Straggling from the gold centre and grieving.

Rapacity and lust will not forbear
And there is no retreat from injury
Except one: *amor vincit omnia*,
And rose and myrtle float in the same sea.

Myrto a woman, Myrtos an island, the Mare
Myrtoum where the rival of Pelops fell.
What light now plays across the sea?
Is there any? O Christmas rose, Noel!

In the Apple-tree

The mistletoe is back
Among the knitted twigs
Of the old apple-tree.
And what is that to me?
My pruning hand still digs
And the old branches crack.

But where the bunch first grew
Is a great skeleton,
The berries and the leaves
For which my heart still grieves,
All, all are gone;
And so I love the new.

How rare now that I can
See new replace the old,
As, on the neighbouring bough,
I see it now!
The pleasure must be told,
And I am still a man.

Deep-rooted Fears

Deep-rooted fears
– Should not fears have deep roots? –
And terrifying love
Send their pale shoots above
The surface where no other growth appears.

Expect no more,
Though other men will live, and women too,
To see out time and witness its distress
And what in us grew less
May grow again as it has grown before.

O barren age! whose trust is all in lies;
Others have known what you no longer know:
Hope backwards, you may find
The speed of a slow mind
Dawdling eternally before surprise.

Wonder there must be which is not short
Or long nor has any dimension.
Can you find that? I say
That there in night shone day
Although I know it only by report.

Leave hope, leave fear, attend to what is,
The smallest thing that is is better than
The best that can be said,
And a man dead
Finds more than we in our short silences.